Benthy

Please return on
A wnewch chi ddych

246: Aftershocks: Stories from the Japan Earthquake #quakebook
Copyright © 2011 Patrick Sherriff All Rights Reserved
Design: Edward Harrison
Cover Design: James White
Typeset in Fanwood Text & League Gothic

Published by Enhanced Editions

307 Westbourne Studios 242 Acklam Road London W10 5JJ

ISBN 978-0-9568-8362-9

2011.03.18 9:13am
Have asked @fatblueman (of Christmas in Japan video fame) to start
writing a song for Japan quake survivors, and it got me thinking...

2011.03.18 9:18am
I want to compile a book of quake experiences and publish it like
within a week and donate all profits to Red Cross We have the
technology.

2011.03.18 9:22am
If everyone wrote 250 words - one page - or submitted their favourite
(original) tweets, pics or artwork, I could edit, publish it in days.

Contents

Names	Yoshiko Ikeda	9
Alive	Steve Nagata	10
Another	Masumi Nabekawa	11
Awakening	Yoko Ono Lennon	13
Beautiful	Christopher Maurer	14
Birthday	Jonas Neergaard-Nielsen	14
Bravery	Yoshie Sherriff	15
Cakes	Arun Vemuri	16
Care	Yuki Watanabe	17
Ceiling-light	Brian Wood	19
Ceremonies	Wesley Cheek	21
Changed	Florian	21
Close	Debora K Ohnishi	21
Contrast	Aurelio Asiain	22
Conversation	Michael Gakuran	23
Cushions	Shaun Hickox	24
Dark	Andy Heather	25
Debris	Greg Harbin	25
Decisions	Ted Taylor	26
Determination	Andy Sharp	27
Disappeared	Brighid Rader	28
Distance	Brent Stirling	29
Encouragement	Grandfather Hibiki	29
Engage	Tokyo Twilighter	30
Escape	James Hou	31
Evacuated	Takamori Hayao	33
Exactly	Mark Rende	36
Expectations	Miho Nishihiro	37
Experience	Kosuke Ishihara	38
Facebook	Joel David Neff	39
Faculty	Rodney Van Meter	39
Forget	Michiko Segawa	41
Forward	Maxamillian John	43
Ganbaro	Lowlypoetic	43
Gesture	N Cobayne	44
Goal	Naomi	44
God	John Janzen	44
Graduation	May Arai	45
Harmony	Tom Hope	46
Heart	Victoria	46
Help	Yui and Shizue Nonaka	47
Home	Kimberly Tierney	48
Illusion	Hiromi Davis	49
Leaving	Sandra Barron	51

Lingering	Soso Bureau staff	53
Lost	Matthew Holmes	53
Loving	Shehan Raban	54
Lucky	Stephen Lyth	54
Muenbotoke	Jake Adelstein	55
Morals	Yuichiro Ito	60
Mountain	Edan Corkill	61
Neighbors	Yumiko Takemoto	62
Normal	Laurent Fintoni	63
OK	Naotoshi Nabekawa	64
Options	Jason Morgan	64
Overwhelmed	Corey Wallace	65
Pajamas	Mark Warschauer	66
Photographs	Mari Aquarian	67
Positive	Arthur Davis	68
Precious	Keiko Fujii	69
Prepared	Annamarie Sasagawa	70
Radioactive	Ian Martin	70
Really?	Chikae Singleton	71
Rebuilding	Mr Salaryman	71
Recovery	Yoko Kobayashi	72
Relief	Don Myles	72
Remoteness	Sybil Murray	73
Same	Baye McNeil	73
Scenarios	Miles Woodroffe	74
Shaken	James Simpson	75
Signs	Terrie Matsuura	76
Strength	Ai Hinton	77
Strong	Robert Ouwehand	77
Television	Richard Smart	77
Together	Jesse Johnson	78
Tremors	Iain Hair	79
Trousers	Joseph Tame	80
Underground	Bigger in Japan	81
Underneath	Yuko Kato	81
Understanding	Mari Kurisato	83
Values	Kaoru Raban	84
Vertical	Philip Brasor	84
Voices	Tomoko Perez	87
Waiting	Kevin Wood	87
Want	Dan Castellano	88
Window	William Gibson	91
Test	Yushi Tabe	92

This book was written as a record of the disaster that befell Japan, as well as a way to provide relief for the survivors. If you received this copy for free, please consider donating to the Japanese Red Cross at www.quakebook.org

Foreword

For me, Tokyo was metropolitan love at first sight. It was 1992, and the government sent me for a language homestay. I got off the Skyliner at Ueno Station from Narita and that was it, I was done for. I could try to tell you why -- the energy of the place, its strangeness, the feeling of method to the madness -- but really, you might as well try to explain your first crush, your first love, the attraction of a lifelong romance. Whatever you can explain in words won't quite be it. The real connection is always too deep, too elusive, too mysterious ever to be corralled by language. The words will never get it right.

Still, if you're in love and you're a writer, you have to try. You might even create a character, say, a half-Japanese, half-American assassin, to help you:

"At first light, the whole of Shibuya feels like a giant sleeping off a hangover. You can still sense the merriment, the heedless laughter of the night before, you can hear it echoed in the strange silences and deserted spaces of the area's twisting backstreets. The drunken voices of karaoke revelers, the unctuous pitches of the club touts, the secret whispers of lovers walking arm in arm, all are departed, but somehow, for just a few evanescent hours in the quiet of early morning, their shadows linger, like ghosts who refuse to believe the night has ended, that there are no more parties to attend."

If my books have been love letters to Japan, this one is an SOS. I'm both proud and humbled to be part of it, to be in a position to reach others who love Japan and long for Japan so that together we can give back some of what we've received, and to do something to help Japan back to her feet.

Barry Eisler

Introduction

The idea for this book came out of desperation; desperation to do something for a country on its knees.

As I write this, intense aftershocks still force me out onto the street with my daughter in my arms, even though we live far from the hardest-hit areas of the country, and far more comfortably than the thousands in refugee shelters.

After nightfall, my city is dark, as we all try to use the least electricity possible to save energy for more important uses. We wear coats in our homes against the cold. We sleep in our clothes in case our homes collapse and we have to run for our lives. We've forbidden our children from drinking tap water for fear of poisoning them with radiation. And we are the lucky ones.

Those of us who live in Japan are in a state of war. But not a war against a nation, or even nature. We are fighting defeat, worry and hopelessness. The question is: Are we strong enough to overcome?

If Japan is to lift itself from disaster, enormous effort will have to be expended by a great many people. Tens of thousands are already working together under extreme pressure toward this goal, in the hardest hit Tohoku region, around the nuclear reactors in Fukushima, and throughout the nation and world. Millions more have donated generously, and wish they could do more.

For the many people around the world who care deeply about Japan, this book is a snapshot of a nation in crisis, told by the people affected, in their own voices.

Our Man in Abiko
Chiba

2011

Linda Yuki Nakanishi

Names

Here is a photograph, dated 13 March, by Kiyomu Tomita, one of the first independent journalists who entered the area after the quake and tsunami. "A girl huddles herself," he tweeted. "She has lost her family. In Nobiru."

I had barely known these place names. Some "bigger" names such as Sendai, Ishinomaki and Rikuzen-Takata were quite familiar, but I didn't know anything about smaller towns. It was just like how I came to know the name Omagh, Northern Ireland, when the Real IRA bomb killed 29 people in 1998. There would have been far better ways to get to know the name of a town or city. The fact is, whether you know the name or not, there are people living there.

How old is she? 11 or 12? I wept, for the first time after the quake. Then I realized that there's another person in the photo. Somebody wearing black socks is sitting right next to her. So, the girl is not alone, at least. I prayed, and remembered the place name "Nobiru." I googled and found it was a famous beach town in Miyagi Prefecture. The girl wore a green top. I shut off my computer.

Another name is "Futaba, Fukushima." On Saturday, 12 March, I went to my local supermarkets. The bigger one was virtually empty. I could buy some ginger though. The smaller store seemed to have had fewer panicked shoppers. They had almost as many kinds of fresh vegetable as usual. Good, I thought, and then I saw the name "Fukushima" on the package of ordinary shungiku. At the time, partial meltdown had already been reported. I bought it. I cooked, praying for the safety of the farmers. It was delicious.

As I found out later, Futaba was where the first cases of radiation were reported. I'm quite sure this is the last time we see a Futaba vegetable at my local supermarket.

Yoshiko Ikeda
West Tokyo

Alive

It's become a ritual that when earthquakes hit Tokyo, people announce on Twitter as soon as they feel them. So I opened up Twitter and sure enough, pages of "Oh, felt that", "Shaking", "Earthquake!" filled my screen. Then things got weird.

As I joined the online crowd, people were commenting on how long it was going on when things started getting rough. The intensity increased and I held onto my desk. I can remember hearing water sloshing around in a bottle inside my refrigerator and thinking to myself, "This is not good." Things fell off my shelves. Everything in my apartment started to move freely. The TV, my china cabinet, bookshelves, even the chair I was sitting in. Honestly, running or hiding never even entered my mind. I felt frozen, watching as things around me were all falling. I felt like it wasn't real. When it was over, it looked like someone had gone on a rampage in my apartment. I was still sitting in my chair, trembling a little.

After a moment I turned back to Twitter and messages were flying past. It was clear now that something huge had just happened. I flipped on the TV and soon learned some of the basics. The quake was centered in the northeast and that we only got a small taste of the full force. People outside of Japan were asking what had happened. News hit of a huge earthquake in Japan, but there were few details. Rummaging through the mess on the floor I found my video camera and a laptop and set up a quick livestream broadcast of the news on TV. For hours I kept the video running as I started to clean up my apartment. I stayed on Twitter throughout the night, as aftershock after aftershock rocked my building, each threatening, then backing down. Soon hundreds of people had logged onto my video as I continued passing information on Twitter to people at work, walking home, or outside of Japan altogether.

I kept at this for the days following, taking few breaks even to sleep as constant aftershocks would soon bring me back to my desk. Together we learned of the tsunami and the terrible damage, the towns washed away into the ocean. Together we learned of the problems with the nuclear reactors in Fukushima. Together we learned that the entire world had heard of the disaster and that planes were on their way to help those in need. Together with thousands of people in my online community, most of whom I have never met, I felt fear, gratitude and sometimes despair, but I never felt alone.

Steve Nagata
Tokyo

Another

When the earthquake struck, I was in the waiting room of a small clinic with my 5-year-old twins. The TV switched over to a broadcast about the quake.

Suddenly the building started to shake violently. I took my children and ran out of the clinic and onto the sidewalk, since I was afraid the building would collapse. Everyone, including doctors, office staff and nurses from the clinic also rushed outside.

The floor above the examination room of the clinic held a rehabilitation center. Elderly folks, blind patients and their physical therapists came quickly out of the emergency exits. The elevators were out of service, so the patients had to rely on the support of young staff members.

As the violent trembling continued, everyone huddled together on the sidewalk. The shaking was so bad that all anyone could do was cling to the ground. My son was so scared that he clutched a nearby tree and held on. Street signals and power lines swayed like crazy. It only lasted for a few minutes but it felt like a very long time.

After everything settled, everyone filed back into the clinic. Just as we arrived, an aftershock came. I grabbed my son's hand and was about to run out again, but I couldn't find my daughter. I told my son to go out without me. As I headed back inside to search for my daughter, one of the doctors appeared carrying her in his arms. Apparently she'd gone back to get my handbag and coat that I'd left behind.

"I can buy another bag or coat, but I can't buy another one of you if you die, so just leave those things behind!" I told her.

Finally, after seeing the doctor and picking up our prescriptions, we walked home. CDs and books were strewn about the living room. Our big, old television set had fallen off the shelf. Everything looked so different that the kids were upset. It was getting late and the air was chilly, but we decided to wait in the garage. I turned on the radio to hear that the trains weren't running. My husband commutes to work by car, so I figured he'd still be able to make it home, but my cell wouldn't connect, I couldn't text and the house phone was dead.

Night fell and it got cold so we went back into the house. My husband called. "I'm fine, but I have to stay and support other workers who can't go home, so I'll be pretty late." Even though it was cold I was too fearful of any aftershocks to use the heater, but hearing from my husband made me feel cozy and warm.

A water main had been damaged in the quake so we couldn't run the tap. Our only choice was to have rice balls for dinner. The kids fell asleep while waiting for daddy to come home. He finally arrived, three hours later than usual. He looked exhausted.

Masumi Nabekawa
Abiko, Chiba

日本地震

2011

Linda Yuki Nakanishi

Awakening

I feel numb now, as if I was there myself and hit with this disaster as you have been. Only just recently I visited Tokyo, and was delighted how beautiful, clean and quiet the city was! I didn't expect a disaster like this to happen to the country I love so much.

One year, John, my husband, Sean and I, were in a hotel in Tokyo. It was in the morning, and the earthquake suddenly hit the three of us. I immediately grabbed Sean, who was still a little boy then. I went into an open closet, holding Sean tightly, and sat in there, kept repeating "Namyohorengekyo". After the earthquake subsided, John laughed and said he didn't understand why I sat in an open closet. I explained to him that it was important to be protected by a structure. Well, at least, that was what I was told when I was a child. The earthquake John, Sean and I experienced was not at all like the one you just experienced. But still my body is now shaking tonight from the memory of it.

So I feel deeply for you for having experienced the earthquake that was the severest in the history of Japan. It must have been so, so horrible. I extend my sympathy and love to each one of you. I'm very sorry that you had to go through what you went through. My heart is with you all the way.

Yoko Ono Lennon
New York City, 11 March 2011

愛する日本のみなさん、私は今、私自身がそこにいて、みなさんと一緒にこの大災害に襲われたように、ぼう然としています。私はつい最近、東京を訪れて、この街がいかに美しく、清潔で、平穏であるかを喜んでいました。私がとても愛しているこの国に、このような大災害が起こることは、まったく予期していませんでした。

ある年、私の夫ジョンとショーンと一緒に東京のホテルにいました。朝のことでした。突然、地震が私たちを襲ったのです。私は当時まだ小さかったショーンをすぐに抱いて、扉が開いたクローゼットの中に入り、しっかりとショーンを抱きしめてうずくまり、南無妙法蓮華経を唱えつづけました。地震がおさまった後、ジョンは笑って、なぜ、私が扉が開いたクローゼットの中に座っていたのか理解できないと言いました。私はそれは、骨組みによって守られるので、重要なことなのだと言いました、少なくとも、私が子どものときに教わったことでした。ジョンとショーンと私が経験した地震は、みなさんが経験したようなものでは、まったくありませんでした。でも、そのときの記憶で私の身体は今、震えています。

日本の歴史上もっとも甚大な被害を及ぼした地震を経験したみなさんのことを、私は深く感じています。どんなに怖かったでしょう。みなさんのおひとり、おひとりに、私のお見舞いの気持ちと愛を伝えさせてください。どうしてこんな怖いことを、みなさんが経験なさらなければならなかったのだと苦しく思います。私の心は、いつでもみなさんとともにあるのだということを知ってください。

愛をこめて、ヨーコ。
オノ・ヨーコ2011年3月11日

Beautiful

In the midst of all the concern and fear, my wife and I received a bit of very happy news: a photo of my mother- and father-in-law. It was taken by my wife's high school friend, who made the long and potentially dangerous drive from Tokyo to their hometown in suburban Sendai. The photo shows our teary Mom and Dad smiling, happy and safe. It's easily the most beautiful photo I've ever seen.

Christopher Maurer
Chicago, Illinois, USA

Christopher Maurer

Birthday

I was working alone in my optics laboratory in Koganei, in a single-story building where quakes are rarely felt. When the shaking started it didn't take me long to sense that this was a Big One. Everywhere around me, equipment was rattling more and more violently and a few small things fell to the floor. I quickly convinced myself that there was no immediate danger of being hit from above and whipped out the mobile phone camera. I filmed the optical table heavily wobbling on its pneumatic vibration damping legs, gas canisters beating against their stands, 19" racks swaying and posters in the hallway swinging synchronously from side to side.

After the shaking had died down, I went outside with people from the other labs and heard over the loudspeakers that the quake had been rated a 7 on the Japanese scale in Miyagi. Back in the lab, with NHK on, I could soon watch in terrified disbelief the destruction wreaked by the tsunami on the northeast coast.

A few hours later I did a superficial inspection of the experiment, turned off the laser and measurement gear and went back to my office. When learning about the total shutdown of public transportation, and being 30 km away from home, I prepared to stay overnight, while my wife was walking ten km to get home to a terrible mess in our 13th floor apartment.

I called my horrified parents, and then sat down with some colleagues for dinner and a beer. Around 3:00, exhausted from following Twitter and watching doom on NHK, I fell asleep on the office floor. It was my 31st birthday.

Jonas Neergaard-Nielsen
Tokyo

Bravery

I know little about the Fukushima 50 as the Japanese media haven't focused on them yet. I don't know if they really volunteered to stay there to complete their mission or they were ordered to stay there because they're too old to have children. Either way, I'm so proud of them, that they're ready to sacrifice their own life to try to save all of us.

I've been telling our daughters when we spot any of the Fukushima 50 on TV that they are the bravest men in the world. The place could explode at any time. I just can't imagine how their families can cope with everyday life. They must be terrified every time they turn on TV.

We still experience some earthquakes everyday and they make me so nervous. Even a tiny rattle frightens me. *This might be the biggest one. This might be it. I don't want to lose my family. I don't want to die.* My heart beats so fast. I just cannot believe it is actually happening to us. It feels like it's never-ending.

But all I can do is send encouragement to the Fukushima 50 and pray for them. We have to believe that the Fukushima 50 will complete their mission and save all of us. I have to believe that every single man can come home to hug their wife and children who have been dying to see them.

Yoshie Sherriff
Abiko, Chiba

Cakes

My daughter, during the earthquake, was in her piano class. Her teacher held her tight while she continued playing "Row row row your boat, gently down the stream."

Most soothing and reassuring were our building's owners who called Neeraja and Hema down for tea and cake, saying, "It's OK, relax, stay indoors, the house is well built and protected."

All this while I was having a swinging time 30 floors above in Yebisu Garden Place Tower with my colleagues. I returned their smiles for the first minute (knowing that the building was one of the safest in Tokyo). But then I was one of the first to dive and duck promptly under my desk.

The building swayed and shook wildly. I dialed Neeraja to check the family's whereabouts then switched the phone off to save them from hearing the screams in the background.

After what seemed like an eternity and an apocalypse—computers strewn, desks swept clean, printers toppled and presentations mixed up—the more seasoned people suggested we march down 30 floors. No rushing of feet or stomping of ground, no racing through or overtaking, just a good old smiling saunter as if going down for a quick cup of coffee.

Outside everyone was gathered in groups looking up at the still-swaying building, posing for pictures (flashing the recognizable V-sign). After 30 minutes of exchanging frustrations over not being able to reach loved ones, I headed home while some of my inimitable colleagues prepared for the 30-flight climb back up to tie up loose ends.

Phones didn't work, a small glitch in an otherwise extraordinarily efficient disaster management system. I had to walk for a while with no taxis stopping. Apparently part of the drill was to keep the roads clear for fire engines, ambulances, police cars and buses. I took a bus (free of charge) and finally reached home. I'd been already slightly assured that the family was safe (I had checked Neeraja's message on Facebook), yet feared the worst for the precious possessions (TV, iPod, Tolly/Kolly/Bolly/Hollywood DVDs).

And what a sight, when I reached the building!

The landlord, Akaishi-san, opened the door, smiled benevolently in his fatherly manner. He bowed politely and said, "Come come come, the tea is hot, and we've got cakes from Holland, which you'll like. Hema-chan likes them very much."

Inside, the only sign of all the drama outside (which was still unfolding, as we had not yet heard about Sendai and the second disaster to hit Japan), was the swinging chandelier and the excited and reassuring voices of my wife and daughter chattering first to Mrs. Akaishi-san and then rushing to me and rattling off their adventures of the day, which will forever be fresh in our memories. Two things stand out: The zen-like demeanor of the Japanese amidst such a huge disaster, and the realization that if there is a place on earth that I want to be with my family and friends (current and extended), when (God forbid) such a disaster ever struck again, then it's this country, Japan.

Arun Vemuri
Tokyo, Japan

Care

I don't know where to start to write... ten days have passed since the earthquake. My parents' house is within 40 km of the Fukushima nuclear plant. They've been told they must stay indoors. Although the house wasn't greatly damaged by the earthquake or tsunami, as the house is built on solid ground, they have to contend with the problem of radiation.

Although this is far from the worst case of losing a family member or home, they have scarcely any information regarding radiation. All they can do is watch news on TV. They don't know really if they are in danger or if they are safe, and fight against an invisible enemy inside the house. Even if they decide to evacuate, they have no gasoline, so they don't know how far they would get. The trains aren't running, either.

My 70-year-old mother refuses to go to a shelter and insists on staying at home. She says she's not bothered by magnitude 3 earthquakes. Even though the government seems to have forgotten her, she is perfectly calm. What is the government doing? Don't they care about the people in Fukushima? When people living towards the coast were confronted with the threat of radiation, the whole town decided to evacuate without waiting for government instructions. Nobody in my hometown will evacuate. Why? What's more, they took in people evacuating from the town next-door, so now they feel they can't evacuate themselves and leave those people behind.

People of the Tohoku region are stoic, compassionate, calm and humble. They have always just dealt with the situation without complaining. Of course they have questions and fears, but they hesitate to show them as they know other people are experiencing far worse.

They don't expect the government will help them, but they've made up their minds to stay here and fight. Rumors about radiation pollution continue to grow. What have we done to deserve this? We are suffering like others in disaster affected areas. The difference is we have an unnatural and unseen danger to deal with. Please don't abandon Fukushima. Please see the reality. Please give us accurate and timely information. Please get this nightmare power station under control as soon as possible. And please know that Fukushima is doing its best.

Yuki Watanabe
Tokyo (hometown Tamura, Fukushima)

Chris MacKenzie

Ceiling-light

I'm sitting here in my high-rise apartment at 5:30 a.m. after being woken up an hour and a half ago by aftershocks of yesterday's big earthquake. The first thing I saw when I woke up was the ceiling-light swaying overhead. Luckily we are safe, thanks to our high-tech apartment building. It sits on some sort of hydraulic system that prevents the building from shaking too violently.

When I got home from the office yesterday, the only sign there had been an earthquake was a puddle of water on the floor from the fish tank. However, the building where I work had a huge crack in the stairwell. We have been in constant sway for the past 15 hours. As I am writing, another aftershock is rocking the building. Many new buildings and skyscrapers are built to withstand such quakes and are probably one of the safest places to be when one occurs.

However, up north they are not so lucky. The quake was stronger up there and many more buildings were damaged. But it was the tsunami that was truly devastating. It was a wall of water marching its way overland destroying everything in its path, incredible to watch on TV. Tokyo was relatively protected by its location at the inner tip of a large bay, but there are no such sheltering bays on the northeast coast of Japan. Most of it is totally exposed to the open Pacific.

This quake was the largest I have experienced in almost ten years in Japan, and from what I hear, the largest pretty much any Tokyoite had ever experienced. We often feel small tremors that gently sway buildings. It is just part of daily life here and people hardly take notice. If you are walking, you probably wouldn't notice one had even hit.

But yesterday's was different. Once my office building started to shake from an aftershock, I knew it was going to be a big one because of the recent quakes in the past week. Yesterday's quake just kept intensifying and intensifying until a couple of us were forced to crouch under our desks. My older office building is not as flexible as my apartment, so the shakes were probably far more violent.

Now, from the relative safety of this apartment, I remember how I quickly left my office and got a taxi to check on things here. The trains and subways were all automatically shut down, so a cab was my only option. I work about 7 km from home even though my office and apartment are both in central Tokyo. The city closed the elevated expressway that snakes through the city, so the city roads were jammed. The first big aftershock happened during the my taxi ride, near the Imperial Palace. It was surreal. The road was heaving up and down and the cars were hopping on it. I felt bad for my taxi driver, who voiced serious worry about his family. Since the cell networks were over capacity, he could not get in contact with them. Eventually, I had to get out a few kilometers from home and walk. Walking was probably quicker anyway.

I finally arrived home but, the elevators were shut down, so I had to walk up 23 flights of stairs. I can look out my window across the street to a much taller skyscraper called the Park Tower, which houses the Park Hyatt Hotel of *Lost in Translation* fame. Hundreds of office workers were forced to stay in their offices overnight since many live out in the suburbs and had no way home. The lights remained on in the tower for the employees. Office towers all over the city were brighter than usual because of all the employees stranded there. The elevators in my building were still out last night when I did the trek downstairs to walk my dog. The sidewalks were packed with people walking home. This constant human train lasted throughout the night. Everyone was calm and polite and took everything in their stride.

The aftershocks have been a constant at night. For several hours after the first major quake, my building felt like it was in continuous, swaying motion. You get kind of paranoid and feel like you are swaying even when nothing seems to be moving. Looking at something hanging or dangling from the ceiling or walls is a good way to tell if a quake is real or not.

While I wait for aftershocks, I keep looking at that hanging ceiling-light.

Brian Wood
Tokyo, Japan

Fernando Ramos

Ceremonies

Friday afternoon and the kids had all graduated. We sat around the teacher's office in *hakama* and suits, the principal in formal tails. I felt it first. I always feel it first. I always jump up and look dazed and everyone will laugh at me when it stops. But it didn't stop and everyone said, "You're right. It's an earthquake."

Someone inside turned on the TV and said, "It's Miyagi." That's far away from us in Kansai, but an English teacher who'd traveled to America to come to my wedding pulled out his phone to call his family in Sendai. "My family is OK, but no one can get a hold of my brother."

Everyone wandered off and changed out of their suits and *hakama*.

On Saturday the first bullet train ever from Kagoshima rolled into Osaka. There had been a ceremony planned, but it was cancelled. My wife's grandfather, a WWII veteran who'd been a lifelong Japan Rail employee, had been waiting for this day for years. He had had his ticket for the first train for months. He told me, "Isn't it terrible about the earthquake. I am old, but I don't feel like dying yet."

Wesley Cheek
Kyoto

Changed

The Tohoku Earthquake didn't affect me physically, but it changed the way I perceive mass media forever.

Florian
Osaka

Close

I am an American-Hungarian living in Japan, married to a Japanese man. I'm from Los Angeles, so earthquakes were usually not a big deal to me. But now, I will never be so flippant about them again.

On Friday, March 11, 2:40-something in the afternoon, I was at home in my apartment in Utsunomiya, Tochigi prefecture (north of Tokyo, south of Sendai). I was rushing about gathering my son's things for baseball practice. I felt the slightest of motion at 2:46 p.m., kind of like the feeling you get when you are jet-lagged and the world starts to sway, but only for a moment.

"Rock and roll," I thought. "Here we go." So I sat down on my couch to wait it out, which is what I usually do when a quake strikes. But it kept getting stronger. The lurching started to get violent, and my windows began vibrating, and the TV started swaying and shimmying towards the edge of the sideboard. The light fixture above my head swung about. The quake kept getting more and more intense, and I wondered vaguely if I should get under the table. By then, the adrenaline had kicked in, and I felt like I was in a dream—yet the motion was all too real. Time seemed to stand still yet rush forward all at once. And I kept thinking, "This is getting weird, it's lasting way too long."

Another big lurch made up my mind for me. I yanked out a chair and crawled under. I started saying the Lord's prayer and hoping the quake would stop.

Once it was over, I realized it was time to get my son's baseball uniform to the school. As I went outside, I saw another mom rushing out with gear in hand. We piled into the van. The sound of sirens filled the air, and the firetrucks and ambulances were rushing madly about. At the school our sons were huddled in the van of another baseball mom. They charged out once they saw us, clearly high on an adrenaline rush of their own. But the school looked different. The principal was out on the grounds and teams of teachers are rushing about checking for damage. The yard was strangely bereft of students—usually some are playing after school. I sensed the principal wanted to talk to me, but there's a language barrier so we just looked at each other. The other mom was telling the boys to hurry up and change. The principal continued to frown at us.

A little after four p.m. the head coach arrived. He was clearly on edge in addition to his usual drill-sergeant demeanor. "Sugoi jishin! (Huge quake!)" he barked at me. I responded, "Kowai! (It was scary!)" Finally the principal decided to cancel baseball practice.

Little did we know about the tragedy that befell the northern region at that time. In Tochigi, the earthquake rated a 6. No major damage—just a broken cup in the sink and a stack of books that fell off my shelf. I didn't realize that the epicenter was up north, and that we'd only experienced the outer ripples. Yet in Tohoku, the truly "huge quake" unleashed a huge, destructive tsunami that wiped out entire towns.

Close, but not that close. Far, but not all that far. There, but for the grace of God...

Debora K. Ohnishi
Utsunomiya, Tochigi

Contrast

Big contrast: While the foreign media is obsessed with Apocalypses, the Japanese people are already talking of rebuilding.

Aurelio Asiain
Kyoto

Conversation

Living safely in the bosom of central Japan, I've only been able to sit and watch in horror from afar. My struggle has been not from the direct effects of the triple disaster, but the spread of information in the media.

On March 11th at 2:46 p.m. the six-storey building where I work began to quiver. After a few minutes, the tremors subsided and everyone in my office went back to work. Twitter, however, was buzzing. My friends in Tokyo were tweeting in shock—the quake had been huge. With no television or radio in the office, I relied on the internet for updates. People pointed cameras at TVs and began live streaming the news. Cell phone pictures of fires began to leak out.

And then the tsunami came. I watched pictures on my monitor of the land turning black as seawater rushed in, crumpling burning houses and swallowing cars. I rushed home to put the television on as soon as I could. Report after report poured in on the worsening situation and Twitter was alive with new, informed people spreading all sorts of news. I decided to start collecting it together—at the very least I thought it might prove helpful for people looking for information on the quake. Before long, it was the wee hours of morning and my article was pages long. But the onslaught of information didn't stop.

The Japanese news channels had set up live streams online and several other blogs had begun disaster information pages. These provided basic survival information, ways to check the phone numbers of friends and relatives, and pages showing all recent earthquakes and places to donate.

The situation continued deteriorating over the following days, particularly at the Fukushima Daiichi Nuclear Power Plant. The foreign press was scrambling, plastering the headlines with alarming words and shocking pictures. Fear mongering over the possibility of another Chernobyl was rampant as was doom-saying about nuclear fallout over Tokyo, which is 200 km south of the affected area.

Misinformation about radiation spread, overshadowing the plight of the people in the stricken areas of northern Japan. Even previously respectable newspapers seemed to be gripped by sensationalism and were not reporting the basic necessary, objective facts.

But something amazing happened on Twitter. Those of us in Japan and able to understand Japanese noticed a stark contrast between the relatively calm Japanese media and the foreign press. We began translating live press conferences of the Chief Cabinet Secretary and linking to official radiation readings posted by the Tokyo Electric Power Company (TEPCO). People with an understanding of nuclear radiation pitched in and started clarifying out our knowledge on the subject. A team of citizen journalists had self-assembled and started disseminating information that was factually correct, balanced, and peer-reviewed. This was a far cry from the reporting by many professional journalists—reporting that was exaggerated and, in some cases, almost bordered on unethical.

I don't claim that the amateur journalists on Twitter were free from bias or ulterior motives. It is easy to imagine ordinary people being driven by heightened ego and a sense of self-fulfillment, or perhaps a desire to rip down the traditional forms of media. I'm sure my own actions as a blogger are not completely selfless. I wonder deep down how much of my motivation came from a true sense of altruism and how much of it from the growing encouragement and acceptance I found in my peers. I'd like to think that the terrible situation unfolding helped us all to move beyond personal interest.

But what this all proved to me is this: Sometimes what starts as a conversation between a few people about a shocking event can flourish into a service truly useful to many.

Michael Gakuran
Nagoya

Cushions

I was teaching my elementary school class when I was interrupted by the ground shaking and an announcement over the PA system telling the kids to get under their desks. The kids did this pretty quickly, though a couple paused for a chat before getting shouted down by the homeroom teacher. This process had happened a couple of times before, one time for a minor quake and another time for a drill, so I didn't think too much of it. But after about a minute, I thought it was a good time to dive under the desk myself at the front of the class.

I'm not sure how long I spent under there. But as the stuff hanging from the walls began to fall around me and the kids gave panicked shouts, all I could think of was the accuracy of the earthquake simulation machine in London's Natural History Museum.

When the quake died down, the kids got up from under their desks and put their seat cushions on their heads. Everyone filed to the playground. The whole thing felt like a fire drill from my own school days. All the classes lined up while teachers took the register. What shocked me was that the kids were so calm about it all. I guess they are well prepared. However, just as we were let back into the school and were walking down the hall, the first of many aftershocks hit.

All the kids sat on the floor quietly. For some reason, there was a fish tank on a desk in the hall. I thought it best to hold on to it to stop it from falling. Parents had begun to gather at the school gate to take the kids home. School was now officially finished for the day.

I returned to the staff room and began to watch the footage of the tsunami on TV. Watching these horrible scenes, I understood that the quiet surreality of my classroom experience was a part of something bigger, something tragically real.

Shaun Hickox
Tokyo

Dark

Family and friends ask me if things have changed in Kyoto since the quake. Well, cafe lights go dark and convenience store shelves are empty. But what hurts is the idea that the earthquakes were like seeing a loved one getting beaten and being unable to stop it. One of the things Kyoto dwellers most look forward to is the "Higashiyama Hanatoro," a long procession of electric lanterns illuminating the streets of Kyoto's eastern area. Every spring, lovers, friends and families bustle excitedly through glowing alleyways.

Except this year.

This year was different. In Kyoto in March there is snow, wind and rain. There are no cherry blossoms. There are lanterns lining the paths and alleys, but they are not lit. Kyoto is on a different electricity grid than eastern Japan, so the city is not so much saving electricity as it is saving money to donate to the recovery. This is largely a symbolic gesture, but its power cannot be underestimated. Tourists and residents alike are struck by the forlorn nature of the Hanatoro this year. There is little romance or celebration. The dark streets and alleys are a mournful sight that tells you Japan is hurting.

Volunteers stand out in the cold for hours, soliciting donations from the few people passing by in the snow. People are smiling and embracing less than usual. Our stoic faces all say we know this is the right thing to do, but in the streets there is a pervasive, palpable sense of loss.

Andy Heather
Kyoto

Debris

As I rode on my bicycle eastward from my home in Taihaku Ward, the scenery grew progressively worse. Near my house, the only damage that could be seen was small cracks in the houses and people waiting patiently for food at convenience stores or groceries. But soon I started to see dirt on the ground, and then I noticed that things were muddy, and then houses with flood damage.

Before long, I hit areas which had been swept away. Huge trees were uprooted, some fallen onto cars, smashing them to bits. I saw cars stacked on other cars. A house in the middle of the street.

Perhaps if I'd gone further, I would have seen more rescue workers. What once was farmland and small communities was now waterlogged and loaded with trash. There were broken houses strewn around me. Rice cookers and hot water kettles half-filled with mud next to brightly colored futons mixed with the debris of broken trees.

I don't know how it's going to be cleaned up. I can't imagine how any of this will ever return to the normal that I remember seeing just a few months ago. Eventually I had to turn around and go home. In just twenty minutes I was in a bustling city center, able to buy a hot water kettle of my own as other residents crowded into the electronics store, all of us trying to replace what was lost.

Greg Harbin
Wakabayashi, Sendai

Greg Harbin

Decisions

I awoke before dawn to get to my early morning yoga class. I swallowed a splash of coffee to fully awaken, then checked my email. A message from my sister asked if my wife's family was OK. I didn't have time then to check the news, but the message made it difficult to concentrate on teaching yoga that morning.

Later that day, I saw the videos of the tsunami rushing in. I watched one video after another, somehow not quite believing the disaster was real. I monitored Facebook updates from friends, because cell phone reception was down and the internet was the only reliable means of communication.

It was unsettling reading friends' posts that said things like, "Where are you? Did you get the kids?" and, "Trains stopped. Walking home. I should be home in seven hours." I imagined my friends walking helplessly through the cold night. At bedtime, I had a hard time falling sleep. When I did, my dreams were filled with images of walls of moving black water.

The next morning, people I cared about were having a rough time. I went to work, but couldn't keep my concentration. My co-workers could see I was upset. I work retail, and that morning my job just seemed so meaningless. My manager let me go home early. By Sunday, we needed to turn off the laptops and go for a walk. The news was becoming less objective and more sensationalistic. I started to rely more on Facebook and Twitter than any media source. The foreign press sickened me. They were playing up stories of fleeing foreigners that drew attention away from the suffering in Fukushima and further north.

As the week went on, our worries shifted to the reactors in Fukushima. At first, the Japanese media said people in Tokyo were slowly losing their minds worrying about radioactivity while they were jolted by aftershock after aftershock. Yet by the following weekend the Japanese media started reporting more mundane things, and in the international media Japan dropped out of the top headlines.

Now, two weeks later, I still sleep disturbed sleep, and occasionally break down in tears. I lived in Japan for 15 years and I am still very emotionally attached to the country. My wife and I want to move back to raise our new baby when he's born, but I am still seriously trying to consider where to live the rest of my life.

Ted Taylor
Santa Fe, New Mexico

Determination

The Hiroshima Peace Memorial Museum is a shrine to the victims of the August 6, 1945 atomic bombing of the city. One of the museum's simplest yet most powerful exhibits is the large "before and after" models of the city, from a bustling regional capital to ashes.

The Google Earth shots of towns and villages in the Tohoku region before and after the cataclysmic quake and tsunami reminded me of this blackest of days in human history.

The only difference is that the devastation of Hiroshima was at the dirty hands of mankind, while the obliteration of those vast swathes of northeastern Japan was caused by the immeasurable force of Mother Nature.

There was nothing local residents could do to prevent the indiscriminate destruction in either case. As it did in Hiroshima and Nagasaki, it will take many years to restore these areas back to any semblance of normalcy. It will also require immense resources and huge reserves of determination.

But people, especially hardy northerners inured to bitterly cold winters, have an inbuilt resilience in times of trouble. Like the victims of the A-bomb, they will form tighter bonds, dig deeper and come through stronger. Before the disaster up north, people just carried on with their lives. In its aftermath, they will strive to build better ones.

Andy Sharp
Yokohama

Disappeared

My friend Mari and her 15 year old daughter Haruko were in Kesennuma, Miyagi prefecture, when the tsunami hit. They managed to stay safe on a building, but they were trapped as the water rushed into the city. When I finally got in contact with Mari two days ago, she told me how they witnessed a neighbor try to hold onto a post to stop from being swept away. The post broke, and the woman disappeared in the water. She hasn't been found yet.

Brighid Rader
Kentucky, USA

Brighid Rader

Distance

I lived in Fukushima City from August 2006 to August 2010, where I worked as an Assistant Language Teacher on the JET Programme. I have since relocated to Ottawa, Ontario.

When I first heard the news of the earthquake and subsequent tsunami I got on Skype and contacted every single person I knew in Japan that I could and asked about their situation: Did they have water, food, gas in their cars? I feared for my friends scattered throughout Fukushima prefecture. I began reading news reports and quickly realized that the situation was indeed dire. Predictions of a nuclear meltdown and references to Chernobyl scared me. I urged all of my friends to leave, regardless of how close or not they were to the Daiichi power plant. They were getting similar urgings from their own family members and loved ones.

In Ottawa, I further immersed myself in coverage of the events in Fukushima, almost completely dropping out of society and spending over 16 hours a day online. I posted things to Facebook so people there could see what I was reading. My friends throughout Fukushima had mixed emotions: some feared for their lives and fled, others were scared but rational and calm. I think the people who stayed calm and positive had the correct approach. Initial reports of impending doom were sensationalist, scaring people in an already stressful situation. And it turns out the sensationalist media reports of instant death were completely contradictory to what nuclear experts were saying.

From NHK and BBC news, I posted Facebook and Twitter updates for the people in Fukushima about the status of gasoline, trains, roads, and the weather. I also posted reactor conditions and articles about the situation, keeping things objective and avoiding the doom-and-gloom of major news outlets. It was incredible to watch how current and former residents of Fukushima helped each other get the information they needed.

By now, some friends have left Fukushima and some are still nearby volunteering and helping. All vow to return. Through Facebook and Twitter, I am grateful I could help the Fukushima community through this difficult time.

Brent Stirling
Ottawa, Ontario

Encouragement

It's been a nightmare of a week. I pray that everyone afflicted in this terrible disaster will soon wake up from this bad dream, but I don't have any words of comfort. As an old man with an old wife, I've put up with a lot this week. But it's nothing compared with the lives of those staying in shelters. Now things have settled down a little, I will attempt to convey the thoughts of the many other elderly people I have spoken with.

For us old folk confused by the scarcity of information, the radio has been our most reliable source of news. Many of us oldies are familiar with the radio and listen to late night broadcasts, with batteries that last a surprisingly long time. While we can use ordinary mobile phone functions, we've barely been able to operate emergency functions. Batteries run out as we fumble with our phones and the vast majority of us have given up trying to use them.

Very few people of my generation use the internet in the first place, and as power is needed to get online, we haven't been able to use it during power cuts. Even if we connect to the net, we're poor at finding the information we want. Naturally, we can't watch television during blackouts.

While we have inadequate access to information, we can ask net-savvy people living near us to get this information for us. For this reason, we are grateful that mobile phones and the Internet provide information. We rely on one company to provide our home with television, internet and telephone services. While we feared that the infrastructure might have collapsed, the services were quickly recovered. We are thankful for this.

The strength of our generation is our experience. While this disaster is unprecedented, similar experiences such as post-war chaos, oil shocks and the 2005 Miyagi earthquake have kept us prepared. Many people also had stocks of emergency supplies.

I pray that old people who are sick or weak can quickly receive medical attention. But rather then telling healthy old folk that you will support them, it would cheer them more to say that you'll strive to get through this together.

To be honest, it has not been comfortable for people aged over 80. Lining up for hours to get water or do some shopping chills us from the tips of our toes up and gives us back pains. But seeing young mothers of small children patiently waiting for their turn and the impressive qualities of young women who use just a calculator to total up the bills for many customers' shopping, gives me the strong conviction that this country will not break under these circumstances.

It's been a while since my wife and I shared activities and fulfilled our respective roles. Our children have encouraged us and this has led to a reconfirmation of our family bonds. We've also received much encouragement from unexpected people.

I've lived for many years. Night has always turned to day and rain has never failed to cease. Conditions have greatly improved during this week, and will get even better next week. It's time to show everyone what the prewar generation is made of. We need to stay strong.

Grandfather Hibiki
Sendai

Engage

People keep asking me what they can do to help Japan. And while I am all about donations, spreading the word, organizing charity events and the like, I realize not everyone has money to give—and no one seems to have the power to stop the media from sensationalizing the stories while ignoring the victims.

To support Japan, what I would say is this: Simply do what you do every day, but do it better. Go to school or to work but with passion and energy. Engage your neighbors or community but with more sympathy and compassion than you ever have. Let these historic moments move you, inspire you and invigorate you for as long as the feeling lasts because, believe me, that initial adrenaline and humanitarian solidarity will wear off. Ride it as long as you can. Let it make you be a better person, and let it wake you up from the complacency in your life.

Tokyo Twilighter
Tokyo

Escape

I'm in the Benimaru supermarket, just reading a message from Aki about what I should buy for dinner. The phone alarm rings as it always does when a large earthquake occurs, but I don't notice it over the noise in the supermarket. The floor starts shaking a little, and everyone stops and waits. It shakes harder, and everyone starts to panic. The workers calmly gather people around, but the force makes it hard to stand and I pull my phone out to mail Aki, fearing this could seem like a movie, but is in fact real.

The ceiling breaks, glasses break, food stands fall, and all I can think of is how not to die. "Don't die here, James, don't die," I say to myself. I hurried outside toward my school to catch my breath, and suddenly the wind blew and snow started to fall. I felt cold, a cold that chilled my heart. My classroom was a mess and strong aftershocks were regularly warning people that this quake wasn't simple. I must have been stupid to think there was a chance I would be going back to work that day. I gathered myself and started walking home for an hour to find Aki.

I was worried. I couldn't reach her because my phone's battery had run out. It turned out she was home trying to clean up our place, which looked as if it had been robbed. When I got there, we gave each other a big hug without saying anything. We tried to clean, but aftershocks left us no choice but to grab the essentials and leave the apartment. Our apartment had cracks everywhere, so we developed a routine of going to the refuge center at night and back home during the day.

After two days, cell phones began to work again, but only barely. Everywhere you went, there were long lines of people trying to gather any food and water they could find. Things in our neighborhood were getting harder while the situation at the Fukushima nuclear power plant deteriorated. We were still not aware how bad the situation really was, since the government wasn't providing much information. To add insult to injury, we also found out that our company stopped paying us the day the quake hit.

So, acting on our instincts, we decided to leave the prefecture. We had heard that some of our "friends" had left already without deciding to tell us. We booked a taxi, knowing the fare to where we were going would be ridiculous, but we didn't care. We

Mari Kurisato

packed very little since we didn't have much time to think and took our cab to Nasushiobara station in Tochigi Prefecture. This was the closest Shinkansen station to Tohoku.

So began our escape from the Tohoku region. And we left without knowing when, or if, we would ever return.

James Hou
Koriyama, Fukushima

Evacuated

I wasn't able to continue writing since my battery died, but I got an adapter at the Apple Store after arriving in Osaka. Yes, we have evacuated.

Yesterday morning I woke up my son early and told him, "We've decided to leave Sendai. Please know that you might not be able to return to this house again. It will be at least a week, maybe a month, or a year before we return. Or maybe never. Start packing your clothes in the school bag. You will not need any of the first grade textbooks nor your notebooks because there will be no more school in March. You can take your baseball gloves with you, but will have to leave behind the bat."

The primary reason for evacuation is our concern over the effects of the radiation exposure on small children, in the event of meltdown at the Fukushima Nuclear Power Plant. I, of course, feel guilty about leaving when I think of our friends who are left behind in Sendai. However, I thought I have to be responsible about my child's future, and not allow him to be exposed by choosing not to evacuate when means are available, not to mention how much I might regret it.

In addition, small children must be prioritized for care and assistance in a disaster area. Parents with small children, therefore, are not able to do much while just being a recipient of the relief aid. For this reason, we also concluded that a family such as ours must evacuate as soon as possible.

When the first explosion happened at the Fukushima Plant, we decided to leave within a week at the most while monitoring the situation. However, Sendai is in complete isolation, with no prospect of reinstatement of the train service at Sendai Station, the airport is completely destroyed, and access to highways is restricted to emergency vehicles only. The only escape route is via Yamagata airport in Yamagata Prefecture and accessible on the regular road. Yesterday on the way to Yamagata, we heard the news of the second explosion on the car radio. We told our son, "We don't think you'll ever be able to go back to Sendai."

Crossing the border into Yamagata, we were shocked to see a different world: traffic lights working and shops open normally. Why was nothing coming into Sendai when there were food and electricity only an hour away, and no access restriction to the regular roads?

In Yamagata, Mayo, my partner, chose to return to Sendai with food, medicine, and other essential supplies. She had been torn, up until our departure, about evacuating while others were left behind. She now strongly insisted on going back. "We don't need two adults for evacuating one child. I know how to drive back. I have so many friends and I'm concerned about their whereabouts. We have just enough gas for driving back to Sendai."

We then called a friend of ours with experience in disaster relief from the Kobe Earthquake, and asked about practical needs at evacuation shelters. So Mayo drove back to Sendai, with our car piled up with various medications, female sanitary goods, heating supplies, and food items that are easy to share and distribute. It has been a difficult, painful separation for me, accompanied by a deep sense of regret as we have gone our own ways.

In fact, upon deciding to leave Sendai, we took all that was left in our home (vegetables, eggs, diesel fuel, etc.) to the nearby evacuation shelter at our son's school. We were told then that no aid had arrived, and saw the profound need for relief goods and supplies. Was I right to just leave when those much-needed goods were right in front of me and I had the ability to transport them to Sendai? I struggle with these questions. And was I right in allowing Mayo to turn back when the situation was going from bad to worse and the evacuation was becoming more difficult with each passing day? Should I also have gone back?

My son and I remained at Yamagata airport and tried to get on a waiting list for one of the emergency flights. But it was extremely crowded (mostly with those returning from business or sightseeing trips in the area) with a long line of people trying to get a number just to be on the waiting list. While standing in the line we were told that all flights were full for the day, and that we needed to come back in the morning to start waiting in the line again for tomorrow's flights. I just prayed that we would be called today and kept staring at our number. Fortunately, we were called at the very last minute for the last flight of the day, and were able to arrive in Osaka that night.

Arriving in Osaka, what we saw from our bus to the city was another world. At Shin-Osaka Station, I felt confused. Did the earthquake happen in the same country? But I was finally able to watch the TV at our hotel, and saw the graphic images of roaring floods and the explosion at the power plant, something I hadn't been able to see under the blackout in Sendai. And I was truly glad at the timing of my son's evacuation when I heard the news of the third reactor in crisis.

At the same time, my thoughts went out to the many children still remaining in Sendai, including our son's classmates, and I was horrified at the worsening situation with no end in sight.

I woke up this morning to the news that things had become even worse and resolved not to return my son to Sendai. It became clear to me that we must help people evacuate from Sendai as quickly as possible, especially families with small children.

Mayo and I are now working to arrange the evacuation for families based on our own experience. We're also exploring options for places to stay in Osaka. Mayo will be traveling to the Kansai area bringing some families with her.

I have a request for all of you. If you know of any families with small children in Sendai, please urge them to leave. I'll write more if I have energy left, but I'd like to

consult my friends in the Kansai area about our evacuation and temporary housing plans. I really appreciate your help.

(Takanori and Mayo have managed to arrange the evacuation for 30 people by chartering two mini-buses. They were to leave Sendai tomorrow.)

Takanori Hayao
Osaka

Exactly

The hardest thing for me, as a father, was that we were all separated when it hit. My wife was at her office, and my two boys were at their schools on opposite sides of the city. That's always the big fear, that we won't be together when the big one comes. I couldn't get through on the phone, so I sent my wife an email and turned on NHK, keeping one eye on my Twitter feed. My older boy arrived home last, after walking the 13 kilometers from his high school. It was only around 8 p.m., but it felt like we'd waited an eternity for him, especially since by then the TV was showing some truly scary footage.

People here in Nihonbashi are calm and pulling together, despite minor inconveniences like limited train service, rolling blackouts, continuing aftershocks, and some bare shelves in the shops. I can't complain, compared to the unimaginable suffering of the survivors and evacuees up north.

I see that I have finished writing this exactly one week after the earthquake hit, at 2:46 on a Friday afternoon.

Mark Rende
Nihonbashi, Tokyo

Mark Rende

Expectations

The great earthquake on March 11th has caused devastation in the Tohoku and Kanto regions, the likes of which has never been seen before. First, I send my condolences to those who have died and to the survivors. I thank the workers fighting hard to minimize the effects of the disaster despite the risk to their own lives, and I wish them a safe return to their families.

In my hometown of Abiko in Chiba prefecture, a quake of grade low-5 on the Japanese scale was recorded, far smaller than near the epicenter. Because we are inland, we did not get any tsunami effect. Nonetheless, it was the biggest earthquake I have ever experienced, and we have suffered greatly. I am a mother of two small children and the innumerable aftershocks worry me. But, above all, my greatest anxiety is caused by the radiation leak from the Fukushima Daiichi nuclear plant.

I think the biggest problem has been in the transfer of information. The only thing I can praise the Tokyo Electric Power Company for is the rapidity and accuracy of reporting radiation levels to the public.

They said at their press conferences that the radiation level was only a few microsieverts per hour. When they explained that amount to the public, they compared their figures with the amounts we're exposed to naturally every year, or the strength of an x-ray. Surely these figures are not comparable because the radiation exposure times are very different? These comparisons have only served to confuse the public and have made the explanations difficult to understand.

Also, we're told that people living over 30 km from the radiation area of the nuclear plant should not be concerned. I don't need to be told the same story over and over again in news reports because I know I am not getting sick here.

What I really want to know is, if the situation worsens, what happens? How is the condition of the nuclear plant going to affect us, how far is the risk going to spread, and what is the possibility of this happening? We need to know this kind of information but almost nobody has told us anything. If we had that info, everyone could consider all the options and be prepared for action, and public panic could be avoided if a worst-case scenario happened. But because we lack information, people evacuated the capital unnecessarily.

Why did we not get any information about the risks? I suspect that there has not been sufficient research into the risks posed by nuclear plants because, in the past, everyone believed the pipe dream that all Japanese nuclear plants are completely safe. Perhaps, as a result, nobody had information about the risks involved until an actual accident happened.

Japan is the earthquake capital of the world and, in this country, it is impossible to think that any construction is completely safe. In describing this earthquake we frequently use the word "unprecedented" but when they designed the nuclear plants, they should have expected the unexpected and built beyond basic specifications.

The tsunami that hit the Fukushima plant may have reached over 14 meters. That is over three times bigger than their specs allowed for.

Records from 1896 show that a tsunami of 38.2 meters hit the Tohoku region after the Meiji-Sanriku earthquake. Following the Showa-Sanriku earthquake in 1933, a tsunami of 28.7 meters was recorded. Considering these figures, the "expectations" for the highest safety standards at the Fukushima nuclear plant were not at all enough.

My wish is that all the electric power companies will learn from this accident and do their utmost to prevent future risks. This accident has given us a good opportunity to take stock of the expansion of the nuclear power plants we Japanese have embraced as a solution to global warming. I hope that, in the future, renewable power sources will supply the bulk of our electricity and we won't depend on nuclear power.

Miho Nishihiro
Abiko, Chiba

Experience

On March 11th at around 2:50 p.m., I was waiting for my boss to join me before heading to a branch office of our company in Tokyo. I'm nearly 40 years old. All my life, whenever an earthquake came I'd always tell myself, "It's no big deal, it'll be over soon."

But this quake was stronger than any I'd experienced before. I began to question reality itself.

I was on the 8th floor of our building, which swayed so violently I couldn't stand up. The decorative plants around the office toppled over. Computers tumbled from desktops. My gut told me that this wasn't a typical quake. I turned on the TV and saw the number "7" (the highest on the Japanese seismic scale) and the word "Miyagi" and cancelled our trip to the branch office. In accordance with company procedures we rushed to the disaster prevention room.

Since I work for a certain telecommunications company, we knew right away that communication systems were badly affected, but since we were far from the epicenter we weren't immediately certain of the entire extent of the damage.

Two days after the quake, the news was filled with images of terrible destruction. We sent dozens of staff members to the hardest hit areas, along with dozens of vans equipped with satellite communication systems.

According to a colleague at the scene, the support crews were working around the clock to restore service. These workers had family members that were missing, yet they threw themselves into their work. Just hearing about their sense of purpose moved me beyond words.

Countless people died in the tsunami.

Several days after the quake, the telecom systems are back up and running. But I'm sure it'll take many years for the areas directly affected by the quake and tsunami to recover. It'll be far longer for the spirits of the survivors who lost their homes and families to fully recover. I'm not sure that this is appropriate to say right now, but this terribly sad and devastating earthquake that has made us reconsider our normally tranquil day-to-day lives was like a warning from Mother Nature.

This disaster has made us appreciate the importance of life, of things, the bonds of family, the things we take for granted in our daily routines. To the victims—I know you're in dire straits, but keep your hopes up! Keep moving forward! If you're alive, you'll experience wonderful things! We're here for you.

Kosuke Ishihara
Abiko, Chiba

Facebook

My first thought was to update my status on Facebook. I wrote, "Mom-in-law & I are OK; house is trashed. Piano was shifted three feet, aquarium is just...gone. Neighbor kids are scared witless and the local construction workers shrugged it off & went back to work. No phones & no power yet. Hope everyone else is OK."

And that was the end of it. I tried to call my wife but couldn't get through. I shrugged it off and went on cleaning, knowing she would get in touch with me as soon as she could.

My phone beeped and I checked it, thinking it would be from my wife. Instead, it was a half-dozen posts from friends on Facebook in Japan relaying either their own "shaken-but-OK" statuses, or worried posts from the United States wanting details. Soon, info began to filter in through Facebook and Twitter and Google news about the earthquake and the following tsunami.

More friends checked in while the earthquake was upgraded from 8.8 to 8.9 and the tsunami was reported as ten meters high in places. Just numbers on a phone screen.

Joel David Neff
Takanezawa, Tochigi

Faculty

"Earthquake," I said quietly. Nobody noticed. Kei kept on talking. Even I wasn't completely sure at first, and I'm pretty quick to pick up on them. "Earthquake, we're having an earthquake," I said, a little louder.

Kei said, "Earthquake?...You're right..." Osamu said "Earthquake? Really?" By this time, we had already been swaying for several seconds.

I was in a faculty meeting, in the newest, most shock-proof building on campus. In Yokohama, we were far from the epicenter, and the building insulated us well from even the worst local shaking. We would not know how serious the devastation was for some time.

"It's getting bigger," someone said. Kusumoto got up, walked across the room and peeked through the blinds. "Electric poles are swaying," he said. I got up and walked across the room to join him.

"It's getting even worse," someone said. "Better get away from the windows." For a group of technical faculty members all accustomed to earthquakes, it was at first a curiosity, never frightening.

"Wow, it's big. This is far away and big…" Comments like that continued for what seemed like several minutes before it calmed down, though such a building sways for a long time and, in your mind, for even longer.

The electricity went out. Then the announcement came to evacuate the building, so we grabbed our jackets and went out. Several of us helped a man in an electric wheelchair, lifting him down the stairs. The building includes a gym and pool, so dozens of kids in Speedos and goggles were forced out into the cold. I handed out a shirt and a fleece I was carrying. They haven't been returned, but if that's my biggest loss, I'm fine.

Only once outside, as aftershocks hit and the first reports filtered in through both official news and those arriving on foot from other parts of campus, did we become aware of how enormous and frightening it had been even in Yokohama, let alone the Tohoku area.

About fifteen minutes after the first shock, I got an email on my cell phone from my wife, letting me know that she was okay, that she had one of our daughters and was getting the other. It would be fifteen hours before we would be able to connect via voice or SMS, but DoCoMo's mail and internet operated sporadically from the beginning. I was able to access Gmail, Facebook and Twitter from my smartphone, enough to get a message to friends who relayed it to my parents in the U.S. Internet connectivity, even if imperfect, proved to be a key lifeline for many people. Several people around me had cell phones capable of receiving low-resolution TV broadcasts, which gave enough information to be scary but did not provide a lot of detail.

I spent a frightening night on a chilly classroom floor, terrified that each new shock might bring a tsunami to the coastline where we live. If so, would my wife and girls have time to escape? Our house would have been swept away if a tsunami hit Kamakura. We are closer to the beach than the thirteenth-century Great Buddha, who sits outside in the weather because his wooden temple was swept away in a tsunami several centuries ago.

Ultimately, I arrived home about twenty hours after the initial shock. I found that many friends and colleagues had taken off on foot right after the quake, arriving at their homes after walking as much as ten hours, then waiting even more for trains and buses to resume. Some of them ended up standing out in the cold overnight. In the end, our story is one of distress, but is nothing compared to the ongoing suffering of those in the Tohoku area. Our thoughts are with them.

Rodney Van Meter
Yokohama

Forget

This is a country of earthquakes but this old woman was surprised. Some aftershocks haven't calmed down yet. We don't know what will happen next with radiation issues. I'm old enough to not have to worry about any radiation effects, but that's not true for young children who have a bright future. I was talking to myself and shook my head. I just could not stop thinking about all the victims from Nagasaki, Hiroshima and Chernobyl.

I gave birth 42 years ago. A couple of days after, there was the big Tokachi earthquake in Hokkaido. It was about 7.8 magnitude, if my memory serves. The shaking didn't stop even when I was breast feeding. I picked up my baby and ran outside from the second floor of my apartment. I remember clearly that I ran under the table and couldn't stop shaking, holding my baby in the middle of the night when the earthquakes started. I told myself every time I felt the shakes that I didn't want to lose my child—I couldn't. All I could do was hold my child in my arms and cry.

The aftershocks then continued for a month or so. When I saw a picture in the newspaper in which some university's buildings in Hakodate had collapsed from the quake, I just couldn't believe it. Can nobody do anything to stop natural disasters? Every time we face a horrible natural disaster, it makes me think that the land, sky, seas, and mountains are exploding in anger. Tsunamis swallowed houses, cars, electric poles, schools, buildings, parents, grandparents, and children so quickly.

I can't express how I feel for the victims and their family. Did they have a happy life? How cruel to lose something so precious to a tsunami. They could not even say goodbye to those they loved. I only hope at least all the bodies can go back to their waiting families.

Is there a God or Buddha? Did all humans rush off in the wrong direction? I wonder if we've been neglecting to love our parents and children and to love nature, and that's why nature is destroying us.

We hear so much sad news of the killing of our own children, own parents, and massacres, it's like a horror movie. Why? What went so wrong? More than ten thousand people's lives were taken. Can't the super technologies we created in this modern world prevent a disaster?

A fisherman I know had a minor tsunami experience in Choshi, Chiba, and he said, "You just can't imagine how beautiful the sea is after the tsunami!" I can't forget his comment.

Michiko Segawa
Chiba

Mari Kurisato

Forward

What will tabloid editors do when the apocalypse doesn't arrive? Each day they conjure new horrors to visit upon Japan and television pundits evoke historic disasters. But each day we can see Japan moving resolutely forward, and so they lose traction. At least for Japan, the apocalypse is definitely not in sight.

Maxamillian John
London

Ganbaro

I was sitting at my desk the afternoon of March 11th when my phone buzzed. That's all that happened.

I broke away from writing reports and picked up my phone to read an email from a friend. My friend said there had been an earthquake, and a tsunami was hitting the Japanese coast. I relayed the news to my wife and kids in the next room. My wife said, "Oh dear," but since earthquakes and tsunami are part of life in Japan, the news wasn't a shock. It was an early spring day in Kyoto. The plum blossoms were reaching full bloom, a good sign that winter is on its way out. I wanted to finish my reports so I could walk to the park with my kids. Taking a break, I went downstairs to make coffee and turned on the TV.

Nothing could have prepared me for what I saw unfolding before my eyes.

I couldn't make sense of the images at first. My eyes had to adjust as if getting used to the dark. What I saw was a wharf and dozens of cars on the Japanese coast being swept away like leaves in a gutter. So many cars. What I saw was almost too big to grasp. It was a movie that didn't seem real.

Of course, it was terrifyingly real. The people of Tohoku had been dealt an unimaginable blow that will require years to recover from. But they will. A word I keep hearing from people in the area is "ganbaro." They say it on the news every night, "ganbaro." I saw it spray painted on the side of a concrete wall in the midst of absolute ruin, "ganbaro." The word that has many nuances but in this case can best be translated as, "Stay strong, stand firm."

"Ganbaro" is a word that is sometimes overused. But not now, not in this place. At this time the people of Tohoku and Fukushima need to keep saying it and keep believing it, because the challenge they face is immense.

Lowlypoetic
Kyoto

Gesture

I live south of Tokyo. I can't write about what it felt like to experience that disaster up north because I simply can't imagine it. But I will say this: The people here are to be admired. From the architects who design the skyscrapers in Tokyo, to first year elementary school children, everybody knows what they should do. People help each other out. People get on with business as usual. The traffic lights in my town went out and a few of the locals took it upon themselves to go out and keep things safe by directing the traffic. A simple gesture. A small gesture. A gesture that wouldn't have crossed my mind.

N. Cobayne
Shizuoka

Goal

Watching the events unfold has shifted my focus in life. My vague goal of visiting Japan has grown stronger. It has become a resolution. I will go to Japan, I'll donate, I'll help in any way possible. If by doing so I can take in even some of the dignity, sense of duty and kindness that the Japanese people have in their core, it will be more than an even exchange.

Naomi,
Canada

God

At first it didn't seem like that big of a deal. We are two hours south of Tokyo, and initial reports were all very conservative, with potential death tolls of under 500 people. We were actually kind of impressed, considering the death toll in Haiti not so very long ago.

But that has all turned out to be very, very wrong. Ten-thousand-plus people dead or missing. Certainly doesn't seem "low," especially when people you know are crying because of lost relatives and friends in the north. Everyone's trying go about life-as-usual, but it's not so easy to do. Today we had a graduation ceremony at my son's school. As soon as the speaker mentioned the disaster, half the place was in tears. The Japanese are very good at "gaman" (quietly enduring hardship), but as an over-expressive foreigner, I find that to be aggravating at times. Seems like a good national cry might be a better idea.

I find it hard to escape a certain sense of dread, like a dark voice in the back of my head that mocks my faith in light of meaningless destruction like this. You can't blame terrorists or human evil. Sometimes the earth just up and kills at random, and like Shusaku

Endo repeated so many times in that haunting novel of his—God is silent.

I made up a fairy tale to make some sense of it. I'd like to believe that the only problem is that our communicators are broken. That once long ago, God had such an intimate relationship with his creation that we'd know long beforehand about any natural irregularities, and always be safely out of the way. Maybe we are just crippled by our inability to hear God, and we live out of step with his creation because of it.

I know some people will be offended by my telling of such children's stories at a time like this, so I'll stop there. Today the panic seems to be getting worse instead of better. No one is sure whether or not we'll be running from a radioactive cloud within the next few days. Frankly, I start to think that Twitter and Facebook are more interesting as a study in human psychology than they are useful sources of clear and true information. And CNN can be even worse with their "possible scenarios."

The question, "What is Truth?" is important on so many levels in a crisis like this.

John Janzen
Japan

Graduation

We'd just come home from my elder daughter's farewell concert, when the unprecedented catastrophe occurred in Tohoku and Kanto. Our small daughter was in the toilet, but the kids' room door was shaking, banging. *That's strange. Her sister is still at school. Is it a ghost? What a silly idea.*

No! It's an earthquake! It's shaking like nothing ever before! It took me about one minute to realise this. And then, straight away, came the blackout. I rushed back to the school to pick up my older daughter. Someone was saying, according to forecasts a huge tsunami is coming, but at this point, I was thinking, "No way!" A neighbouring granny said, "We're going to be all right here, dear. If something happens, we all escape together." The neighbourhood agreed.

And then the lights came back. We saw the devastation, and wept. The huge black tsunami, swelling over the levee, swallowing homes and cars in its path. On the Chiba coast, an oil refinery was in flames, spewing bursts of fire.

I couldn't reach my mother. She wasn't answering her mail. Morning came, and finally, a friend living a couple of houses down from my parents told me mum was OK. Daddy got on a train when it finally started moving, came home in the morning, and fell asleep straight away. A friend sent me a message saying she walked all the way home. And then came the worries over the nuclear power plant, people scavenging batteries and non-perishables.

The university shut down as it was spring break anyway. A British colleague is taking refuge at our house. She has a granddad in New Zealand. She's pretty worn out what with one quake after another.

The rollover blackouts are indeed inconvenient, but they're nothing compared to the cold in the shelters. The cake shop didn't open on our little girl's birthday, so I did the baking. For the chocolate, I gathered all the Hershey's left from Valentine's and melted them. Finished baking exactly 10 minutes before the rolling blackout. Phew. We put emergency candles on the gateau chocolat, and together celebrated the little one's eighth birthday.

On the same day, navy-colored slip-on shoes arrived. I'd ordered them for the graduation ceremony. Our usual delivery man from Sagawa brought it. He never stopped his rounds, saying Sagawa will deliver no matter what. I thanked him from the bottom of my heart. "Thanks to you, I can wear new shoes for the graduation ceremony." The ceremony took place right in the middle of the blackout. But it was such a bright, sunny day, there was ample light inside the gymnasium. When the children paraded into the gym, backs straight, chests out, my eyes stung. There was no microphone or anything. Just the fifth-grade children playing instruments and singing songs for the departing sixth-graders. Everything seemed really solemn and holy. Everyone had their heads held high. Twelve-year-olds. How are they taking in this disaster?

The future of Japan will be theirs to rebuild. It will be up to their generation. We weren't sure whether there would be a graduation ceremony at all. I think of how fortunate I am to have been there at such a milestone event. Happy graduation. May you all have a good journey as you walk along your paths of life.

May Arai
Kamakura

Harmony

We were in Kofukuji, Nara, when it hit. It wasn't really much there, but we still felt the tremor. My parents were visiting us on holiday from England and at first the creaking temple was amusing, mum thinking it interesting that old temples creak in the wind. "But it isn't windy," I said. I was the first to realize it was an earthquake and told the others. Then the famously beautiful buddhist statues started rocking in harmony. We jumped out of the temple, only then realizing that standing under the eaves may be more dangerous than inside. But the swaying was gentle in Nara.

Tom Hope
Tokyo

Heart

Sitting around the dinner table earlier in half darkness, watching the latest press conference about exposed fuel rods at Fukushima No. 2 power station 247 km north of here, I asked the gathered Japanese housemates what they would do if the problems there worsened. One of them replied that her family lives in Fukushima, about 60 km from the troubled plant. I suggested that she would be safer here than returning home. She told me that if her family were exposed to the radiation she would return home to be with them, irrespective of the consequences for herself. "That's the heart of Japan, isn't it?" she said. This was met with a chorus of "Yes, that's right."

Yes, it is. To an extent, that's why I came here, why my life is here. It's why even now I don't want to leave. To leave is to abandon, yes? This is a critical time for Japan. Where do my loyalties lie? But I have been researching a route to Fukuoka, 1,100 km south of Tokyo. By the time things get worse, and by the time they actually tell anyone about it—in the absence of independent radiation monitoring by some impartial international agency, if one actually exists—it would probably be too late to make any difference. But I might pack a bag just in case. I've already had one half-packed for the past three days.

I was actually thinking about having a relaxing early night, perhaps finally getting around to that post-move shopping in Ikebukuro tomorrow if the trains were running. This is the surreal contradiction we're experiencing. Here in the house, they're talking now about which male idol has the most attractive face. In the background, experts from Tokyo University continue to discuss the melting-down reactors, and what to do if you're exposed to ionizing radiation. I know which conversation I'd rather be listening to.

Victoria
Tokyo

Help

I feel really sad to know that the tsunami and the earthquakes took so many people's lives. When I watched the news on TV, I thought to myself, "Is it really happening in Japan?" I become very sad each time I see the destruction.

I've been considering what I can do to help. I decided not to waste electricity and water. I'll try to save the important things. I hope that Japan can find joy again soon.

Yui Nonaka (age 12)
Abiko, Chiba

I was with my 4-year-old daughter at home when the earthquakes hit. We were upstairs and I ran back downstairs holding my child since the shakes had gotten stronger and stronger.

I switched the TV on to find out what was happening. There were lots of aftershocks and a second big one. I was so scared and didn't know what to do.

I picked up my daughter and moved to our garden and hunched down in a ball. I certainly didn't expect to have two quakes in a row. I was really worried about my family. I rang and rang and tried to email, but didn't work for some time.

At last I received an email from my husband confirming he was OK. I headed to the primary school where my two other daughters were.

We've never had this scary shaking before. Lots of people who worked in Tokyo could not come back on the day as all public transportation stopped. Nature is terrifyingly powerful. All the victims are now trying to revive their life and towns.

I can't think of any particular things to help at the moment but I will find something one day and try the best I can.

Shizue Nonaka
Abiko, Chiba

Home

Walking up the street to Yoyogi Station from my office, I passed a Starbucks and thought "Oh, double cappuccino? Mmm... No, I just gotta get home—so much to do today." Yoyogi crossing was crowded, when suddenly the concrete rolled and I got pitched forward. Instantly everything was a blur of seasickness, shaking buildings and traffic lights. The pole I grabbed to steady myself, everything nearby in fact, started shaking like crazy.

Traffic halted. A girl crouched down in the middle of the intersection. My sluggish brain told me I wasn't fainting or having a stroke and that this was a big, very big, earthquake. Earth....QUAKE!! I let go of the vibrating pole. Windows were about to blow out of the buildings because they were shaking so badly. I asked myself, "Should I run for it?"

Then it stopped. Japanese announcements came over the public loudspeakers telling people not to panic. I was frozen in front of a convenience store while texting my husband. "Big earthquake, really scary," I told him. "I'm OK—you?" The loudspeaker announcer said "6.0" and exclamations of "whoa" and "ahhh" rose out of the crowd. My text message to my husband failed. I tried to call but couldn't get through. The only thing working was the internet.

So, at 2:49 PM I posted on Facebook, "Big quake in Japan near Tokyo, it's pretty bad, but I am ok. No cell service, no trains. I'm at work." But at this point, as it was after the Towers went down in New York, I knew that things were going to get crazy. A determined energy collected in my gut. I said to myself, "I've just gotta get home." So I started walking, merging into a stream of hundreds of people, thousands. They were mostly dressed in suits, stepping on each other's heels.

In the crowd I walked a long time and saw some odd things. For example, Captain Jack Sparrow was on Meiji-dori for some reason holding a gift bag. At Shibuya Station I was pretty sure there was no way to get a cab. I kept telling myself, "Just keep going... gotta get home." Later, I ran into an actor friend of mine. We walked on together, chatting about showbiz until we got to Meguro Station. Here she kept walking and I waited another hour for a bus to Shinagawa Station. But it was utter chaos as a woman's voice announced: "We are now closing so please go home or someplace else. The trains are not running and we don't know about tomorrow." At this point I had hopes of finding a bus or even a cab, but the taxi line was two bodies deep and hundreds of people long.

So I kept walking. Alone, but surrounded by the hundreds of others, each one of us walking and thinking, "I just gotta get home."

Kimberly Tierney
Tokyo

Illusion

I was at my job when I saw the news of the earthquake, followed by an announcement from city hall warning of a tsunami coming in around 4:30 p.m. We were told not to go near the ocean.

It was around 3:30 p.m. I wondered where my seven-year-old daughter was. I looked for her around our house. I also went to her friend's house, but it was empty. I went to city hall to look for them, but they weren't there. But when I went to the elementary school I found her playing there. I was only looking for 30 minutes, but it seemed longer and I was really relieved when I found her.

Gradually people started wandering up to the school. The next announcement told us that a small tsunami had arrived. Calculating that there would be enough time before another might hit, I decided to go home immediately. My husband was already there, along with my friend and her one-year-old son. They live near the beach so she was very nervous and decided to stay at my house. Although we live close to the ocean, our house is located on a cliff 30 meters above sea level, so we reckoned we should be safe.

We followed news of the earthquake, but things kept getting worse and worse. Continuous earthquakes meant a constant risk of tsunami for people like us who live near the ocean. When one tsunami is expected you can take the appropriate action and then carry on, but now we had to be on continuous alert and that was exhausting. Around 10:30 p.m., there was another announcement that the danger level was upgraded and we were warned of a big tsunami. We stayed up late into the night, listening to the multitude of announcements on the public address system. In the end a 1.5 meter tsunami hit, which luckily caused no real problems for the town.

After what seemed like a very long weekend, I went back to work and asked my students where they had stayed after the big tsunami warning. To my surprise, most answered they had stayed at home. One kid said, "All of my family was watching TV as usual. I live right next to the ocean. I am brave, aren't I?"

Local people have become used to natural disasters and warnings, and most of the time experience tells them the worst case won't happen. Therefore, their minds don't switch to real emergency mode. The friend who stayed at my house said old people laughed at her when she said she was moving to higher ground. What is this laid-back attitude?

日本地震

2011

Linda Yuki Nakanishi

I was particularly shocked to find quite a lot of families didn't evacuate even though they had small children. I cannot imagine what's going on in those people's heads. They think they will be OK because "experienced" older people say it should be OK? For me, it seems like something bordering on superstitious belief. I want the older people to be more sensible, not to be optimistic to the extent of stupidity! Most of the inhabitants of my town are old and the power of old people is still strong.

I overheard some high school kids chatting. They were boasting of how little they or their family had been bothered by the tsunami alert. I was so frustrated and told them, "You don't need to panic and run around in circles, but you should run up the hill!" Every individual needs to take responsibility for their own life.

Why don't parents teach this to their kids?

Japanese people are good at not thinking about the worst-case scenario. They stop thinking. To stop thinking is easy. To stop thinking is safe, because it is the same as everyone else! I think that's an illusion! It is not safe!

Hiromi Davis
Tosashimizu, Kochi

Leaving

A Twitter exchange I saw a few days after the earthquake:

"Anything a returning gaijin can bring back that would be helpful?"

"People who run away don't need to bother bringing back anything—including themselves."

Rice and milk may be in short supply, but there has been no lack of accusations and vitriol in the foreign community following the quake. Those who stay are brave loyalists; those who leave are turncoat cowards. There are as many reasons to stay or go as there are suitcases. Tokyo is my home now, and I wanted to be there to do what I could. I'm not scared of radiation or inconvenience. I walked toward the burning World Trade Center on 9/11. Running away isn't normally what I do. I have a close friend who works at Tepco Systems in Tokyo—she didn't leave. Abandoning friends isn't normally what I do either.

Yet here I am, on a borrowed couch in L.A. I didn't have an answer compelling enough to stand up to frightened family who demanded my "solid reasons" to stay. It's hard to stand up to 1 a.m. phone calls asking, "Leaving is easy, so WHY are you making us all worry like this?" Circumstances did make it easy for us to leave. Since I can work from anywhere, it came down to balancing a remote but tangible threat against abstract ideals.

So I left a key behind hoping that someone who truly needs our apartment will use it. I comfort myself knowing that we are one less household drawing power and two fewer stomachs taking food and water that is desperately needed up north. I don't think my reasons for leaving are any more valid than someone who just felt nervous. Everyone has to do what's best for them. When we were talking about it the night before we decided, I considered that the worry suffered by my family would take more years off their lives than radiation could from mine. All I had to fall back on, finally, was the belief that leaving would damage my idea of who I am. Jim agreed, but asked if that was worth possibly putting my life at risk.

Part of me is glad to be where the only radiation threat is from the constant sunshine. My family is certainly relieved I left Japan. And if that's not worth it, what is?

Sandra Barron
Los Angeles

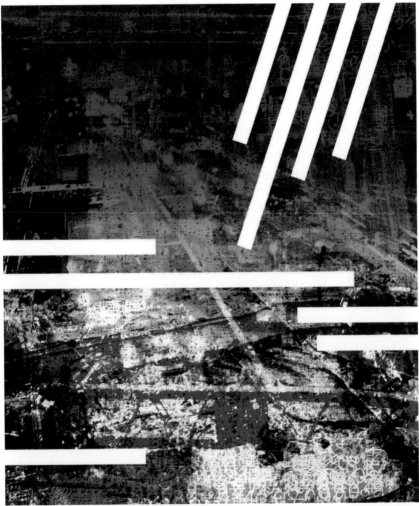

Mari Kurisato

Lingering

It's been a week since the Great Earthquake hit us at 2:46 p.m. on March 11. Our region of Soso has now been designated as an area of radioactive contamination, meaning that we have to head outside the 30-kilometer exclusion zone from the nuclear plant to pick up relief supplies.

Many people from Fukushima Prefecture have had to evacuate, but many still remain. Many haven't relocated because they are too old to move to emergency shelters.

Many linger because of their deep attachment to the land handed down from their forefathers.

Medical workers, working in devastated facilities with extreme shortages of medicine, also remain to help the many people who need them. Local government officials stick around to fulfill their duty to protect residents until the government orders them to evacuate.

We pray deeply for all the victims, and as remaining residents, we vow to protect our beloved cities.

Stay strong, Soso.
Stay strong, Fukushima.
Stay strong, Tohoku.

Soso Bureau staff,
Soma and Futaba cities.

Lost

I am not the person you are looking for or, indeed, the story. This exchange is not between rescue-worker and missing person, parent and child, embassy and ex-pat, but journalist searching for a tale of woe here in Tokyo, of all places. I could give them an angle, yes, and an account of what was happening or had happened to me, no problem, but the "grim reality" was that here, life pretty much carried on.

My thoughts are with those in the north and east of the country, and those around the country (and world) who have lost family members and friends.

Matthew Holmes
Shimokitazawa

Loving

Though I have lived nearly nine years in Japan, I have experienced many earthquakes that have not frightened me. March 11th was my first time to be frightened.

As I took leave from work to go to the doctors, things didn't go as well as I had planned. I'd only gotten ready to go at around 2:30 p.m. As my son came home after school, I waited a little longer until he settled down with his homework.

Then suddenly the earthquake struck.

As everyone probably thought, I thought it would end soon, but it didn't. It became more furious the more time passed. I saw things shaking vigorously around and falling. Even the building was shaking (as we are on the fifth floor) and it made me frightened. I told my son to put on a jacket and we ran outside for safety.

We were safe outside. We returned home after about two hours. Thank God that everyone was safe. At home, on the news, the real truth of the disaster unfolded. The tragedies that have happened to innocent people are too much to bear. The earthquake, the tsunami and then the nuclear power plant radiation.

Since we're safe, it taught me a good lesson about life. The importance of loving and taking care of your loved ones when they are alive. It can be family, neighbors, friends, or relations. As natural disasters can happen anywhere at any time, we should all be loving, friendly and happy while we are alive.

Shehan Raban
Kohoku, Chiba

Lucky

I was in Shinagawa, Tokyo, in a meeting on the 19th floor. I wondered if this would be the end of me. The sounds were unnerving—not just rattling and banging, but loud creaking and groaning. We had a panoramic view across the city and over Tokyo Bay. Across the street we could see other skyscrapers swaying like palm trees in the breeze. Fires sprung up in various places and huge plumes of black smoke rose from Odaiba.

Had the quake stopped? The building kept moving for ages. Worried about my girlfriend, I peered anxiously down the coast towards the towers of Yokohama Thermal Power Station, looking for smoke. None. But across the bay in Chiba, vast, terrifying explosions could be seen on the horizon.

We decided to stay where we were because we were in a relatively safe building, at least if a tsunami hit Tokyo Bay. Our meeting continued for the next three hours, interrupted by several big aftershocks. I can't remember anything that was discussed. I had motion sickness from the constant swaying.

Eventually, my girlfriend rang from home. She had walked. I took that as my cue. I descended the many flights of stairs and joined an orderly pedestrian exodus along the

Stephen Lyth

old Tokaido Highway. After a while, I passed people gathered around a TV that an old lady had set up outside her shop. Only then, seeing the aftermath of the tsunami, did I realize how serious this really was and how lucky we were to be in Tokyo.

Stephen Lyth
Tokyo

Muenbotoke

On March 11th, 2011, an earthquake of almost unprecedented magnitude...

Last year I had my palm read, for a lark. It was part of an event at a boutique hotel—wine, cheese, and a palm reader. The woman doing it seemed pleasant enough, maybe early forties, long black curly hair, wearing a long red skirt, leather jacket over a purple blouse, an Egyptian ankh necklace with a thin black silk rope holding it around her neck instead of a chain.

She cheerfully took my palm in her hand as I sat down, and as we made small talk she honed in on my palm, slightly pushing the palm with her tiny, thin finger and said something a little odd. "You have a square in the mount of Mercury. You will lead and have lead an exciting life shadowed by fatality wherever you have been and will go."

"Couldn't I get a slightly cheerier reading?" I quipped and she laughed and I pretended to have to meet someone, that I was late, and I left.

I don't need someone to tell me that life involves fatality. We all know that amusing little Buddhist proverb on why we are mortal: "The cause of death is birth."

True. Death is part of my business. That's the extreme end of being a crime reporter or an investigative reporter.

For many the coming of spring is symbolic of birth, rebirth, vitality. For me, it used be a reminder that a lot of people are going to start dying and I'll be busy. People are a little less active in the fall and winter—the cold slows them down, cools down tempers, bodies don't rot quickly, the odor doesn't give away their secrets. But by the early spring or late summer, what's killed rots quickly and what's been laying dormant begins to stink. The heat makes temperature and tempers rise, anger flares in sync with the solar spots on the sun. Hot tempers lead to fatal mistakes, impulsive murders, rape, arson, lethal assaults. Hasty attempts to cover up crimes don't go so well. The missing are uncovered and/or their deaths known much faster.

Please don't think as a reporter that I dreaded the summer. Death is always a good story. It's always tragic.

....devastated Japan. Thousands died and thousands are missing. It was a natural disaster compounded by a partially man-made disaster, the collapse of a nuclear power plant in Fukushima Prefecture.

However, as a reporter in Japan, it's not just enough to find a tragic event to write about—it has to be a good tragic event. There are plenty to choose from. Sometimes, however, a tragedy is just a plain tragedy.

In 1999, covering the 4th District of the TMPD was an interesting assignment. There was enough crime and sleaze in Kabukicho alone to keep me busy, but I had to cover a wide area and a lot of police stations. The Totsuka Police station was one of them.

On a weekend in July, the body of a sixty-two year old man and his fifty-nine year old wife, Mr. and Mrs. Akutagawa, were found dead in their apartment. It looked like a double suicide or in Japanese what they call "*murishinju.*" *Shinju* in medieval times meant a suicide pact between a man and his lover, or even a family. *Muri* means unreasonable in Japanese and together the term refers to a suicide/murder in which one persons kills a loved one(s) and then him or herself. Yamamoto had asked me to go talk to the police and see if I could get a human interest story out of it.

I went to the home of Mr. and Mrs. Akutagawa before going to the police station. The door was slightly open, so you could see into the place. The apartment was filthy, totally covered in trash. Newspapers, magazines, clothes, randomly strewn about and a TV on the floor. The neighbors had stuck close to ten notices on the door asking them to clear the hallway and the area in front of their apartment.

Empty plastic bowls of ramen were stacked outside the door. The postbox was filled with bills.

I went to the Totsuka police station but they didn't have much to tell me. One cop did break protocol and showed me photos of the couple.

In the photo of the crime scene, a towel was placed over Mrs. Akutagawa's face, and there were no signs that she put up a fight at the time of her death. As background information on the incident, the detective working the case told me the couple not only had outstanding loans on their condominium apartment, but likely held a significantly large sum of consumer debt as well. Probably borrowed money from loan sharks.

They'd drunk poison. The husband had boiled a pack of cigarettes, Peace or Hope brand, in some alcohol and water. There was enough nicotine in a pack of cigarettes that if you distilled it and drank it down, it could kill you very quickly. She'd died first and he died shortly afterwards. I gathered that death had been quick. Painless or not, I didn't know.

The assistant chief told me, "He was a faithful salary man that had just been laid off, and had just started at a new job, then that didn't work out. It happens like that. A guy gets put in a situation where even when living a relatively simple way of life, a man can't save enough to repay loans and this eventually this leads to suicide becoming an apparent solution to the problem. It's evident that the guy was not skilled in money matters and didn't know how to handle his finances. Gambling was most likely involved."

Many of the staff at the nuclear power plant stayed on the job long after radiation levels had risen past even the laxest of safety standards, to prevent a full melt-down. Why?

"You can call it double suicide, but if he killed his wife without her consent, it's murder. He should be prosecuted for it accordingly with all facts investigated and necessary paperwork submitted."

The cops do this in Japan a lot; they file papers on dead perpetrators. Just because you're dead doesn't mean the wheels of justice stop turning.

I tried to flesh out a story by talking to people who knew the man, but no one did. I had gotten a photo of the guy from the police. I thought that would be helpful. It wasn't. He was practically invisible. Akutagawa was temporarily employed at a construction company located in the Shinagawa Ward of Tokyo. If he had any friends or acquaintances in the area, no such individual having a close relationship with Mr. Akutagawa could be identified.

The female managing the apartment complex stated, "I didn't have a personal relationship with the man, though he has seemed a bit strange recently. I didn't notice any indications of ruckus related to debt collection." When she was told that the man may have had a heavy loan burden, she commented, "It could be true. It does seem that he enjoyed pinball and gambling, but I just really can't say for sure. We're not supposed to speak about that in public or to the media, even if it was true."

It's because they are willing to give their lives to save the lives of thousands of other people, people they know, people they don't know, and people they will never meet.

Another resident of the complex, a middle-aged woman working part-time said, "We were living in the same apartment building, but I never got to know him. I may have met him before, but I can't place his face. Since I've moved into this complex, I haven't gotten acquainted much with those living around me. Yesterday, I was told that the wife of the person living in Room 201 died, and thought that it must've been a double suicide. It wasn't. She just killed herself. It probably would've been helpful if she had someone to confide in, but it seems that she had no one she could talk to."

Questioning the owner of a Japanese pub next door resulted in, "I'm not familiar with the man. If he was a customer, I'd mostly likely recognize his name."

On the first floor of the complex was a beauty salon, but questioning was not possible due to Tuesday being the salon's off day. An attempt to gain further clues from speaking with someone in the salon was set for the following day, as was a visit with the elderly woman working at the nearby ramen shop which I hoped would give me something to go on. I came back the next day. No luck.

It's amazing to me that people can live in an apartment complex right next to each other for years and not know each other at all, not even in passing. This was the case with the Akutagawa family. They had no friends, no social life or interaction with the neighbors. Mr. Akutagawa lost his job, they ran out of money, and they made a suicide pact. A lot of Japanese people hate to ask others for help—even from close friends.

That was the whole story. All they could tell me at Mr. Akutagawa's former company was that he worked hard and didn't talk much. Work was slow, they had to let people go and Mr. Akutagawa wasn't young or fast or particularly good at building. So they laid him off. He'd only been working there a few weeks.

Those who are still working there may survive a few weeks, a few months, but the unseen radiation they were exposed to has probably already killed them. They are living yet already amongst the deceased.

I went back to the Totsuka police and asked them if they had found anything else about the husband and wife or the circumstances leading up to the suicide. The detective showed me the note he had left behind. It was addressed to no one—they didn't have any children.

The note said simply: "Don't worry about us. We've been dead for a long time. Sorry we didn't clean up before we left. We didn't have the energy."

Very Japanese, very apologetic.

The police had found some very nasty letters from a consumer loan company, Yamaguchi-gumi backed, in the mailbox of Akutagawa. Debt collectors had also shown up at his workplace. He was apparently being threatened and harassed at regular intervals. Still, the suicide couldn't really be blamed on the loan sharks. Not in a criminal justice sense, the detective told me.

I asked when the funeral was going to be held and where but they didn't have anyone claiming the body. They were *muenbotoke*, literally, Buddhas without connections. There was no one to mourn for them. There was no one who would miss them, pine for them. At least not in Tokyo. There would be an ad put in the paper, and if no one came forward, the cremated ashes would be transferred to a temple on the outskirts of the megalopolis.

The detective asked me if I could write something in the paper but I didn't have

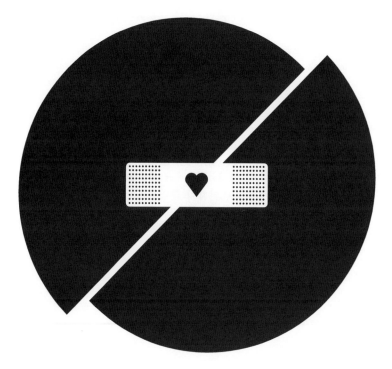

HLP JPN

Gavin Strange

much for a story. I told him as much. He nodded.

I asked him where the temple was. I checked back with him two weeks later. The ashes had been moved there. I took a cab to the temple the same day, and the priest showed me where they housed the ashes. I'm not sure I remember it correctly but there were about three stories of urns in the pagoda dedicated to the *muenbotoke*. On one floor, there were the ashes of children and infants—people who had had loved ones. Someone had stuck a photo of one child onto his urn. A cute kid, little round face with big lips, fuzzy eyebrows (for a Japanese kid). He had on a navy blue Hanshin Tigers baseball cap in the picture.

The priest took me to where Mr. and Mrs. Akutagawa had been put to rest. I lit a stick of incense, put my hands together, mumbled the only Buddhist prayer I could remember and left.

By now, the ashes of the Akutagawas have probably been evicted or displaced by the ashes of other *muenbotoke*. This happens. When family members don't pay the upkeep fees on gravestones and burial plots in Japan, the remains are moved and new tenants are sought. Even the dead can only rent in Tokyo.

I think I'll still visit the temple this summer anyway and pay my respects to the Akutagawas before even the memory of their memory is gone. It seems like the least I could do. Everybody needs someone to mourn them. I hope that when my time comes, there's someone who will do the same for me. I couldn't tell you why that's even important to me but it is.

May their memories last longer than the accident that took their lives. Because remembering them is all we can do for them now and for all those who lost their lives. And in that act of remembering, hopefully we will lead better lives and remember to care for all living things. We owe the dead that much.

Jake Adelstein
Tokyo

Originally published in Shambhala Sun, rewritten for #quakebook.

Morals

It's been one week since the evacuation. Yesterday we found 260,000 yen in cash under the rubble. Our shelter has 150 people in it. Looks like we'll be here for a while yet. We all discussed what to do with the money. Everybody agreed to take it all to the police station. I'm proud to say that we decided that lowering our moral standards would be too terrible, even during such a great emergency. We survivors are left to consider what makes us who we are, and what needs to be protected at all costs.

PS: Thank you very much for leaving lots of comments. I'm relieved to know we're still connected to the rest of the world. I'll try to gather more information from Miyagi.

Yuichiro Ito
Kesennuma, Miyagi

Mountain

I remember the moment I first looked at the Zushi City tsunami hazard map. It was after we'd moved here. I enlarged the map on my computer screen, traced the road to our house and found that it was partly covered by a rude green splotch indicating up to 50 cm of flooding. The map-makers had postulated a maximum tsunami of five meters. I guessed that in a worst case scenario we'd end up with the ocean gently lapping at our doorstep, kind of like when a large wave races up the beach and soaks just a corner of your towel.

This memory flashed before my eyes at exactly 3:36pm on Friday, March 11. I know the time precisely because it was also at this time that I sent an email to my wife: "Climb the mountain," I wrote. "Escape!" By then, about 45 minutes had passed since the earthquake, and I hadn't once got through to her mobile or our landline. In those 45 minutes the tsunami warnings for the Miura Peninsula, where Zushi is located, had grown more urgent by the minute. Monitoring the television in my office in Tokyo I had first seen predictions of a 50 cm wave, then one meter. Next, they said three meters. Zushi was shifted from the orange category to red: "tsunami" to "major tsunami."

"This was it," I thought. "The real thing."

I tried again and again to call my wife, but it was hopeless. With the tone of a dead line still thumping in my ear, I stood in front of the television at work. NHK was broadcasting images from up north. What I saw wasn't a gentle lapping, nothing like it. A massive wave was rolling over houses and buildings like they were sandcastles. Large fishing boats were being thrown through barns several hundred meters from the sea. Then, as if they knew I was watching, NHK cut to their revised list of tsunami warnings.

Miura Peninsula, it said, "Six meters."

I was shaking as I bashed out another email. "Climb the mountain. Take the emergency radio. Listen to it. Climb the mountain," I wrote. Like the first email, this one received no response. The only real precaution I'd taken in choosing where in our seaside idyll we'd rent a house was to make sure we'd be near high ground. Our house is about 20 meters from the foot of the high-wooded ridge that divides Zushi from neighboring Hayama. Hop a fence, cross the neighbor's garden and you're at a path leading up the "mountain," as we call it. I was praying my wife had already gone.

With the Zushi City Government website down, I turned to Twitter for local updates. There I learned that the city had been in a blackout since the quake. No one could make calls in or out. Someone had tweeted, however, that the sea was receding rapidly at

Enoshima. "I've never seen it this low," they wrote. Enoshima is about 10 kilometers west of our house. I remembered that the mobile phone carrier my wife and I used operated a disaster message board. I registered myself and checked if my wife had done the same. She hadn't. Back on Twitter I realized that I wasn't alone in seeking information about Zushi. There were dozens of tweets echoing my own desire for information. "Anyone who knows what's happening at Sakurayama, Zushi, please tweet," said one. I hit retweet. Sakurayama is where we live.

Scrolling through the tweets, I noticed that most were from men. Most seemed to be in Tokyo. Most were at work. I wondered if they, too, had been the ones in their families to suggest living by the sea. I wondered if they'd done so because they wanted to surf, sail, fish or just walk along the beach every now and again. I wondered if they, too, now felt responsible for endangering the people they loved most.

The authorities had only made plans for a five-meter tsunami. I hadn't even done that. NHK's tsunami warning for Zushi still stood at six meters. I kept following Twitter looking for information on whether it had hit. I found nothing.

I did a Google transit search and plugged in the Tokyo district where my office is located, and Zushi. On its default "train journey" setting it came back with a travel time of 80 minutes. All the trains had stopped, so I switched to "walking journey" mode. Ten hours, it said. Like many of my colleagues, I was about to spend a night in the office. I tried to think about work, about how we should respond to this, how this was going to affect what we had planned. But I couldn't. I couldn't concentrate. I couldn't stop thinking about what might be happening at home, to my wife. I couldn't, that is, until 6:40 p.m.

I know the time because there's an email in my "sent" box with that time stamp. It's addressed to my father, and it explains that I had just managed to get in contact with my wife. "She climbed the mountain," it says. "Now she's moved to the public library with our neighbors and she'll stay there tonight. No major tsunami has hit Zushi, yet."

Edan Corkill
Zushi, Kanagawa

Neighbors

We lost all of our lifelines immediately after the earthquake. We had no idea what had happened as we were unable to use our cell phones or watch TV. We were so scared that we just could not stay inside of our home that night. We chose to stay in our car. There were aftershocks, one after another throughout the night, preventing us from getting any sleep.

It was not until two days later that the electricity in our house finally came back on. The gas came on soon after. I can't describe how happy and lucky we felt to eat warm food under the bright light. We had not been able to drink much liquid for the past two days, so the coffee we were having that day was especially tasty.

It's now ten days after the earthquake, and we still do not have running water in our house. However, I think about how lucky we are to still have that house. Especially since there are a lot of people here in Ibaraki whose hometowns are in Fukushima Prefecture and who still have not been able to contact their families.

We managed to carry on with our lives without running water. Our neighbors provided us with water from a well in their garden. They also gave us some drinking water, instant noodles and some dishes to use for meals. I honestly think we could not have done anything without their help. I told them that words could not express how much we appreciated their help. They told me, "You'd do the same thing if we were in trouble." I'm so grateful for the kindness we received, from neighbors who provided well water to strangers, who shared their water to fill out our bathtub.

My neighbors' kindness reminded me that it is very important to stay connected with our neighbors, and to help each other. I would like to urge everybody to be more actively involved in their local community in their everyday life. Because nobody can survive without the support from others.

Yumiko Takemoto
Hitachinaka, Ibaraki

Normal

In the space of one week I've been through fear, sadness, paranoia, anger, tiredness and euphoria—each day bringing with it more or less a different feeling. Until today, when I stepped out to have a cigarette and coffee and for the first time in a week felt as if everything was normal. No wind, sun shining, warm air, people going about their business in Koenji as usual.

Laurent Fintoni
Koenji, Tokyo

Fernando Ramos

OK

More than 6,000 people have passed away, and many more are not found yet. Many survivors lost their homes and are living in the gym as shelter. There is not enough food, water or heating oil.

One of the nuclear plants has been damaged. It is very serious. It's very close to meltdown. And the weather is still cold.

I'm OK, but it's a pity for the children. Sometimes the electric power is cut off. Gas stations are closed and trains do not come as usual. But we are OK. We are living. Please do not worry about me, please worry about people in the north.

It's cold, but I'm OK. Keep in touch.

Naotoshi Nabekawa
Abiko, Chiba

Options

The most surprising thing for me was that my life never flashed before my eyes. Other than the twenty or so minutes during which I couldn't get hold of my wife to check if she and my daughter were safe, I like to think I didn't really panic or feel much fear. My co-workers might like to differ, but this is my story and I'm going to make myself seem brave.

I was at work in Tama Centre, Tokyo, preparing for a day of lessons. I teach English at an *eikaiwa* where most of the students are kids, along with a few near-mute adolescents and assorted adults thrown in for good measure. All five of the school's teachers were together when the quake struck.

We fled the building and decamped to a nearby car park right under the Tama Monorail, which at that point was swaying like it was made of rubber, and screeching. One co-worker advised us to pray. The rest of us tried to get signals on our phones so we could call loved ones. We had all figured out pretty quickly that the quake was big, and that somewhere people were suffering.

I spent the next few days glued to the computer, while my wife's family was glued to the TV. Slowly but surely, news about the tsunami was overtaken by panicked reporting on the nuclear reactor problems in Fukushima. And that's when the e-mails started from home.

"Please come home", "We will pay" and "You have options" were common themes, but never once did I want to leave. This is my home. It is a country I love. It is where my daughter was born and where I met my wife. It is the only place I have enjoyed working, and I couldn't pack it in just because the chips were down.

Jason Morgan
Kawasaki

Overwhelmed

Am I supremely lucky or cursedly unlucky? Neither I nor my immediate family have been in harm's way for even one second. Friends and extended family—even while at risk—have come through mostly fine. But I have experienced from afar the destruction of the two places in the world that I call home.

I've never been a good one for specific times and dates. However 12:51 p.m., February 22, and 2:46 p.m., March 11 will always stick in mind. Christchurch and Tohoku. Earthquakes are nothing unusual to either country. Neither is it unusual to have a friend or two overreact to such events on Facebook. The TV went on. But placid, boring old Christchurch looked like a war zone—the sort of place that is anywhere but Christchurch.

At 6:46 p.m. New Zealand time on March 11, I was getting ready to head home for dinner. I was about to close Twitter and the same flood of concern from Japan was overwhelming. My wife is from Fukushima City and my son was born there. Fukushima City was my Japanese home, and Sendai, as my frequent weekend host, was my second Japanese home. My sister-in-law lives there with her husband and young son. I called my wife. She said, "If you are calling about an earthquake it must be quite serious."

At that moment NHK started showing that dreadful, dark and irrepressible wave heading towards the outskirts of Sendai. "Yes, I think it's quite serious. I'm pretty sure

Lee Chapman

I am watching a tsunami hit Sendai. Maybe Fukushima City is fine, but make sure your sister is not dithering around in some shopping mall!" The wave kept going and going. I had always had this idea of a tsunami being akin to Hokusai's Wave of Kanagawa—a massive thing that rises out of the water, has a huge impact as it hits land but quickly recedes after its short-term but destructive energy is spent. Not so.

As I write this there is a massive torrential downpour outside. Suddenly the water dripping from the roof, soaking the carpet of our central Auckland home doesn't seem to be such a big deal.

Corey Wallace
Auckland, New Zealand

Pajamas

Keiko, my wife, was alone in her ninth floor office at Waseda University in the center of Tokyo when the earthquake hit at 2:46 p.m. on March 11th. After several minutes, she was able to come out from under her desk and run down the nine flights of stairs to the outside.

She first ran to our apartment building and up six flights of stairs to our apartment, where our six-year-old son was with a babysitter and Keiko's mom. Our son Danny was quite scared and was comforted throughout the entire earthquake by the babysitter. Things had fallen in the apartment but there was no structural damage.

They all walked downstairs to wait in the lobby while Keiko ran to the kindergarten/day care center where our five-year-old twins were. She had to ring the buzzer a long time before the teachers heard it over the commotion and let her in. Kids were in pajamas and bare feet, having been awakened from their naps. The teachers were getting their shoes on and getting ready to evacuate everyone to a nearby open space.

Keiko took our twins and walked home with them. We suspect that the teachers and many of the children ended up sleeping at the school that night because, with trains shut down in Tokyo, parents may have been unable to arrive from work. My whole family—Keiko, the three kids, grandma, and the babysitter—walked back upstairs to our apartment. Surprisingly, power, water and local phone service were all working. Long-distance phone service, however, was not available.

Since she lives far away, our babysitter was stranded. She spent six nights at our apartment, the first night alone in the front bedroom and the other five nights huddled in the back bedroom with the rest of the family. With aftershocks hitting every few minutes—some the size of good-sized earthquakes themselves—it was difficult for everyone to sleep.

It is Saturday morning in Tokyo now, and my family is still in the apartment. Fortunately, we have enough food to last for a while. Elevators are still not working. We are trying to decide whether to remain hunkered down all day in the apartment or venture out to the park and playground a few blocks away. The kids are doing well today, though,

Andrew Woolner

in the living room in their pajamas. They're disappointed that their favorite Saturday morning cartoons have been usurped by 24-hour news broadcasts.

Mark Warschauer
Tokyo

Photographs

I've never been to Japan. My Japanese mother didn't tell me much of her family when she was alive. I have many photographs of her family—brothers, sisters-in-law, nieces, nephews, great-nieces and great-nephews. My mother died in 2000, and I have all of her letters and photographs. The letters I cannot read, and I know only two of the faces in the photos for sure—my aunt and uncle. My son is very curious about his Japanese heritage and wants us to visit. I have been slow in thinking about how to go about that. How to communicate.

The morning of March 11, 2011, I awoke at 5 a.m. and switched on the radio to listen and stretch before arising. I heard the news of an earthquake and tsunami in Miyagi prefecture and my heart jumped as I leapt out of bed and turned on my computer. I knew the name of that place, because of the return addresses on those letters. The addresses were the only parts written in text that I could read.

For a week now, I obsessively read Twitter messages, read stories, look for pictures and video online—all in a hopeless effort to know that the people in my mother's photographs are OK. I may never know. I worry and fret. I donate money. I want to wrap up in safety those people who loved my mother in another country. I'm hiring a translator to help me find them. I could have done that a year ago.

I'm ashamed that it took this disaster to motivate me to try and make contact with my Japanese cousins. I regret letting so many years pass by with no effort made. My mother had a favorite niece she spoke about when I was still a girl. I hope it's not too late to meet her. My son is studying Japanese. I hope it's not too late.

I love Japan. Something about it feels like home.

Mari Aquarian
Concord, New Hampshire, USA

Positive

March 18 2011. I switched the TV on yesterday morning before going to school for class and I wished I hadn't.

I can't get the image out of my head:

The TV crew just happened to be there at that moment.

A boy (maybe 10 years old) was looking through the wreckage of a tsunami-ravaged town with his aunt and grandfather.

The grandfather came running out from a wrecked building—he'd found the missing mother's car.

The boy looked so excited.

Like somehow everything was going to be OK.

Like some miracle was about to happen.

The aunt screamed and ran into the building followed by the boy and TV cameraman. She looked again at the car's numberplate and called out her sister's name. The car had been forced up towards the ceiling of what might have been a car park. The woman climbed up and put her palms on the window of the car.

She could see her sister strapped into the car that had been swept into a building by the tsunami and called her name again.

Still the boy's expression was filled with hope, he didn't understand.

His mother was found...everything was going to be all right, phone the police, phone for an ambulance everything was going to be OK...

He didn't realize...

Face filled with hope.

I couldn't watch anymore. In half an hour I would be in class at elementary school and I would need to be positive: Teaching 10-year-old kids, showing them what an exciting and fun world was waiting for them.

Arthur Davis
Tosashimizu, Kochi

Precious

It was 10 minutes before our daughter was due to arrive back from her kindergarten by school bus. The earthquake started and got stronger and stronger. Suddenly the TV died and all the furniture started shaking. Lots of things fell from the bookshelves and the fridge door opened. I was at home by myself and told myself, "I'm scared. I'm scared."

I could not calm down after the big earthquake and headed to the bus stop to pick up my daughter. The school bus didn't arrive on time and I couldn't get hold of my husband at work nor my daughter's kindergarten. Much, much later, the red bus carrying my daughter came. I was so relieved I couldn't stop crying when I found she and her friends were all safe. We were too scared to go back into our house and so were our neighbors. We decided to stay outside together for a while.

I managed to get hold of my husband at that time. I still remember clearly how grateful I was that we were all alive. Later that night we finally contacted our parents in Tochigi and heard that everybody was fine. I learned from the news that lots of people lost their families and houses in the tsunami.

It's not just somebody's story, as a mother, to know that many people lost their precious children and many children lost their parents in such a short time. If there is anything I can do to help, I am happy to contribute. I only hope that all the survivors can stay strong and feel happier about life soon.

Keiko Fujii
Abiko, Chiba

Philipp Christoph Tautz

Prepared

At 2:46 p.m. on March 11, 2011, I was at home in Tokyo's Shinjuku ward, writing an abstract to a research paper I'd just completed. Our apartment started to shake. I thought, "Oh come on, not now, I'm trying to concentrate. Abstracts are tough."

You get used to earthquakes in Tokyo. The city rumbles every now and then but the shaking rarely lasts more than a minute. This time, it kept going. It got stronger. I shut my laptop and went to stand in the doorway. The shaking got even stronger. I started to think that standing in front of a glass door wasn't the best thing to do, so I stood under the steel frame of our front door and watched the skyscrapers in our neighborhood wobble.

I know I wasn't the only one thinking, by then, that this was the big one. I know I'm not the only one who followed that thought with the silent protest, "But I'm not prepared!"

There was an emergency earthquake kit under our bed. A list of emergency landline numbers by our phone. A childhood's worth of earthquake drills in my memory. I had prepared, yes, but I wasn't prepared.

Annamarie Sasagawa
Shinjuku, Tokyo

Radioactive

I'm in a small club in Koenji, drinking beer with a group of 20 or so young Tokyoites. A man in a hard hat and face mask is conducting a mini orchestra of vintage 1980s synthesizers.

Beneath the cheer and good humor, however, they are only too aware of the new uncertainty that Japan is facing. The man's getup is just one of the eerie reminders of the tragedy that had struck northeastern Japan less than a week ago. His father was from Fukushima, close to the nuclear power plant, and the band's drummer also hails from the same area. There are smiles and laughs around the room when Kraftwerk's 1975 song "Radioactivity" comes on in the background, but it's a dark, ironic sort of humour on display, rarely seen in Japan.

A small TV in the corner remains tuned to NHK, Japan's national broadcaster, and all eyes turn to the screen. An aftershock has been recorded near Tokyo. Here in our Koenji basement, no one felt a thing, but as numbers recording the strength of the tremor start to appear on the onscreen map, a cheer goes up among some of the people present; the Koenji area scored 4, putting it in the level of most extreme shaking. There's a sense of victory: we took the worst of that tremor and didn't even feel it.

The party goes on. For now.

Ian Martin
Tokyo

Really?

Pour cereal. Check email. Check the online news. WHAT! Is this for real? What the hell is going on? Can't find any in-depth info on the Canadian news websites. The American news articles are frightening. I settle on reading tweets from a live blog on an Australian news website. At least those tweeters are actually there.

I feel helpless. Why don't I feel safe even though I'm miles away? I'm worried about my relatives. I'm worried about the evacuees. I'm worried about the nuclear plant workers.

I go to Facebook to see everyone else's reactions.

Baby pictures. Ski trips. Weddings.

Really?

Chikae Singleton
Calgary, Alberta, Canada

Rebuilding

Exactly one week after the disaster and it's a sunny day, albeit a bit chilly. Spring is supposed to return in force soon and get the Tokyo temperatures up to almost 20 degrees. As gasoline is still hard to get, my family and I headed out on foot today to get some groceries at the local supermarket. Things almost seem back to normal. All the small shops close to our house are open for business. To our great joy the fantastic-but-expensive local bakery is open, which allows us to get hold of some good bread for the first time in a week. The supermarket is reasonably well stocked and we manage to get some diapers and the other stuff we need, even though toilet paper, tissue paper and rice are still sold out.

The situation in the Fukushima plant is still worrisome, but the worst doomsday advocates seem to have calmed down a little bit. Perhaps this is because the reality is bad enough, and the foreign media has switched its reporting to the situation in Libya and other, more dramatic news stories.

Minor aftershocks keep on coming, but the frequency and intensity are growing less. They hardly grab my attention as long as I know my wife and baby are safe with me. Rolling blackouts still affect the greater Tokyo area, but power hasn't been interrupted where I live. Maybe they have forgotten our secluded little valley, or it is sitting on some big, secret thing we don't know about that needs constant power. You never know.

But as I write this, there is also the sense of a return to "normalcy." I'm drinking a beer and finally relaxing after a week of constantly trying to learn more about the situation, about earthquakes, about tsunami, about radiation and about the extent of death in this tragedy. I know that strong aftershocks will follow, but I am okay with that. It doesn't mean this whole thing will repeat itself. For now, I can relax a bit for the first time in what feels like an eternity. I think next I'll enjoy a large whiskey.

Perhaps we're seeing the end of the disaster and the start of the rebuilding.

Mr Salaryman
Tokyo

Recovery

I have seen images of the disaster area that was affected by the tsunami caused by the eastern Japan great earthquake. I have no words to describe the dreadful scenes.

I'm experiencing for the first time empty shelves at supermarkets and gasoline stations with no gasoline, all because of the two big earthquakes and aftershocks. The radiation from the nuclear power plant makes me nervous because you can't see it. There is a lack of electricity. I can only hope that when I save electricity it helps others.

I pray for a quick recovery as soon as possible, and that we never have a disaster as great as this again.

Yoko Kobayashi
Abiko, Chiba

Relief

"What a ridiculous time to be awake," I groaned to myself. I had only gone to bed three hours earlier, but a dull ache in my left knee left me restless.

Looking at my Twitter stream I failed to see any significance in a tweet which arrived from my friend in Japan. Indeed, I'm sure neither of us realized what a massive understatement the phrase "That was a big aftershock" was at the time.

Shortly afterwards, other tweets started to appear from news organizations reporting the quake, but nothing seemed extraordinary. I didn't give much thought to what seemed to be a standard post-earthquake tsunami warning.

It was much later at work when people started to contact me to see if I'd heard from my friend in Japan. I took a quick glance at the BBC and I saw an image of the devastation for the first time. I instantly returned to Twitter to check that my friend was OK. Thankfully, he'd been one of the lucky ones, with family nearby. They were reunited quickly, with none of the uncertainty which plagued so many others.

Relieved, I went back to the BBC. Dark sludge made its way across farmland. This wasn't the bright blue sea I remembered from videos of the 2004 tsunami. This one looked far more sinister. It didn't stop. I kept waiting for it to retreat, as a wave is supposed to do. But this wasn't a tidal wave, this was a TSUNAMI and it swallowed everything in its path.

Now I am left with a pang of guilt. As I watched footage of the dark water swallowing up entire communities my overwhelming emotion was that of relief. Relief that my friend and his family were safe.

Don Myles
Falkirk, Scotland

Remoteness

I won't forget the first video I saw of the tsunami. This black mass rolled over the landscape, gulping, chewing and spitting out everything in its path. I waited for the ebb to come, but it didn't. The black water just kept going and going. I reversed the video and hit pause, staring at the scene frozen on my computer screen. I was frozen, too.

Even with video, it is hard to comprehend the speed of the event and the noise that huge volume of water surging past must have made. The people in front of it must have felt hunted, terrified that they couldn't escape. In seven minutes of video the whole landscape disappeared. They started tallying the death toll. One dead, then thirty-seven, then... Hundreds, thousands. Here in the UK, it struck me that these people were dying without ever knowing if their loved ones survived.

There was more video, of course, of the aftermath. It showed boats where cars should be, cars where people should be and very few people at all. I saw some tearful survivor reunions, which caused me to cry. I know, I have no right to these emotions in my geographic remoteness, but I do feel for them, too.

Sybil Murray
United Kingdom

Same

I was walking toward Kikuna station in Yokohama. As soon as I entered the station I saw two cops running towards me, and they were looking up instead of at me. I followed their eyes and saw that the power lines and poles were swinging. In fact, everything was swinging and shaking! That's when my legs got wobbly, like I had a sudden charley horse. But I stayed cool. Eight years in Japan and I was used to the terrestrial hiccups that occur here almost daily. And these tremors are usually pretty short. You can forget they even happened in a matter of moments.

But, as I looked around trying to keep my balance, I realized this was not a tremor. In addition to the power lines and poles, the train station and surrounding buildings were shaking! I heard loud noises, rattling, clanging, banging metal and glass like a thousand chandeliers shaking. Sounds I'd never heard before were coming from all over.

It was like the street was screaming.

I staggered out of the station to the sidewalk. Traffic was still moving since some motorists seemed unaware of what was happening. I groped for a building wall to lean on, and as I looked above my head I saw a sign swinging on flimsy hinges. All around me were things that could kill me if they fell. Structures had become lethal. The dry cleaner's nearby, for example, was literally a shaking, swaying two-storey ton of bricks. I spotted what I thought was a safe place to run, but I changed my mind when a window there exploded into a shower of glass.

But through all this, there were no screams. There probably would be anywhere else, but there were none in Yokohama.

For a moment, I looked around into the silent faces of nearby Japanese people. Normally, they were strangers to me, people I usually hold in contempt. But despite my uneasy relationship with them, in that moment I felt no spite, no disgust, no animosity and no contempt for them nor from them. For the first time in years we were one and the same! They looked at me and saw a person, a very scared person, not some foreigner to be feared.

It was an amazing moment. The people around me and I had shared something I would not immediately discard. Finally, after eight years in Japan, that short time made the Japanese my kin. And I realized how sweet and fragile and the same we all are. The temblors stopped and I went into a coffee shop next to Kikuna station. I sat down and watched the unflappable old-timers sip coffee and read their newspapers.

I smiled, and sat there resting and feeling very Asian.

Baye McNeil
Yokohama, Kanagawa

Scenarios

I'm sure everyone is reading scary reports about the radiation situation in Japan in the foreign press, and yes, it is most definitely a serious situation in the vicinity of the plant. I'm following the information extremely closely. Still, based on US, UK and Japanese governments and science officials, there is no risk in the Tokyo area currently.

If this situation changes, we will of course take appropriate action immediately, but at this time, we are safe here, 200 km away. Sadly, a side effect of the wonderful immediacy that Twitter and Facebook bring us is that as much misinformation seems to propagate as real info, and in these circumstances, it's so easy to panic.

The foreign media in the US, UK and France are also not helping. I wish they'd put as much effort into raising awareness, support and donations for those currently affected by the tsunami who are without food and shelter as they are now putting into producing Hollywood-esque nightmare scenarios or segments about how iPad 2 sales are impacted by this. Please.

This situation is being defined by the heroism of those working on-site at the power stations and those providing critical support in the areas devastated by the tsunami. Please direct all your concerns and warmest wishes in their direction.

Miles Woodroffe
Tokyo

Shaken

It was the most terrifying day of my life. The country came to a standstill. My wife walked home for nearly eight hours in her new shoes, about 20 kilometers, arriving home just before midnight with a fellow refugee in tow. Being home was comforting, but it was not the end.

That first night was infinitely more terrifying than the initial earthquake. Aftershocks hit time after time, little shakes and big bumps, each time forcing us to question whether it was time to flee the building.

We started the night with just a single emergency rucksack on standby at the entrance, but by early morning we'd assembled two further bags with clothes and blankets—the basic essentials that might make a disaster a little bit more comfortable.

Every creak, every muscle spasm, every electronic beep from the television set us into flight mode. While there were few major aftershocks in the daytime, as night descended that thick tension set in once more, confirmed by a large aftershock, as occurred every night that week.

James Simpson
Kawasaki

Andrew Woolner

Signs

Three days before the earthquake, my dog—who has slept upstairs in my son's room ever since he was a puppy—refused to go up. If we took him per usual, he'd whine and scratch at the door all night and no amount of taking him outside for one final pee or presenting him with a tasty rawhide treat to gnaw on changed his mind.

A little before noon on March 11, while sitting at my kitchen table drinking coffee with friends, several crows dropped from the sky and began making a huge ruckus in my front yard. It was a weird moment. So striking that one of my friends exclaimed it was like a scene from a horror movie.

It's silly, I know, but I've always been on the look-out for signs. I live in Shizuoka Prefecture—over 400 km southwest of the Tohoku Pacific Earthquake—and we are long overdue for our own magnitude 8-or-above tremblor. Last year my city even gave out emergency radios that automatically switch on and give early (by mere seconds) warning if a large quake is coming. Earthquakes are, and always have been, on people's minds here.

However, despite years of watching cloud formations, keeping an eye out for earthworms fleeing to the surface and observing the newts I keep in my foyer, I completely missed the fighting crows and the dog's reluctance to go upstairs. (Yeah, I know, whether those two things are related to the earthquake up north at all is anyone's guess.) It's just something I did: looked for signs of impending doom.

When the Tohoku Pacific Earthquake actually hit, the dog was sleeping on the sofa and the birds outside were quiet. Lamps swayed, pictures rattled against the walls and the house creaked and moaned. It wasn't until I turned on the TV that I learned the epicenter was up north and the devastation was incomprehensible, even at that early stage. It was a true horror show.

On March 16th we had a magnitude 6.4 earthquake in Shizuoka Prefecture. I began sleeping in my coat with a flashlight in the pocket and suspecting every wind-blown creak of the house was our Big One. I'm as prepared as I can be, but I realize I cannot keep focusing on the negative. It's so easy to get overwhelmed with the devastation—the earthquake, the tsunami, and the nuclear plant in Fukushima.

I've decided to change strategies. I've started looking for more encouraging signs, anything that inspires hope. It's been a little over a week since the Tohoku Pacific Earthquake. The birds are back to normal, but the dog still refuses to go upstairs. He prefers to spend the night downstairs with the cats, sometimes in the litter box. It's a very small thing and I'm sure it will take awhile, but I am looking forward to the day when he makes his way back upstairs to sleep at the foot of my son's bed.

Terrie Matsuura,
Shizuoka

Strength

Each time I see the devastation on TV, my heart aches and I can't stop crying. I saw an old woman on TV one day say, "The crying stage has already past. From today, we don't have any time to cry. There are so many people who suffer much more than I do."

Even while trying to accept that she has to face this terrifying situation and move forward, she still remembers to care for others. That is the true strength of people. I only hope that all the victims can spend some peaceful time with their precious loved ones as soon as possible, and that their smiles will soon be back.

Ai Hinton
Kashiwa, Chiba

Strong

Here in South Korea, talking about Japan can be tricky.

During colonial times, a group of Korean women were taken from their homes to provide sexual services for Japanese soldiers. They were called "comfort women," the nicest possible way to say "sex slave." Every Wednesday, the survivors, very old now, still stage demonstrations in downtown Seoul, demanding the Japanese government recognize their plight, and pay reparations. They have lived hard lives: many were unable to have normal lives afterwards because of the stain on their pasts.

Of all people, these "comfort women" wouldn't be blamed for drawing some satisfaction from Japan's misfortune, yet they set aside their old hurts, and held up signs of comfort and consolation to Japan: "Be strong."

Robert Ouwehand
Seoul, South Korea

Television

It passed through my head that I may be mistaken. Perhaps my neighbor was indulging in some afternoon lovemaking. While the ground in earthquakes often sways from side to side, it seemed to be going up and down.

And then it got serious. I grabbed the flat screen television to prevent it from hitting the ground as a wine glass fell. Luckily, I'm messy—it landed on a jumper strewn across the floor.

And then it got violent again. I dove under the table, unsure whether what I was doing was correct. My backside was sticking out from under the table. If the ceiling came through, would I be paralyzed by falling rubble? I started to shake as the tremors failed to subside. I live within earshot of the Yamanote Line that circles Tokyo, and I could hear a cacophony of announcements competing with the city council. This was the sound of an earthquake.

Finally, the intensity subsided. I got out from under the table and left the house. All the stairways and elevators were inaccessible. Leaving via the fire escape, when I got outside I saw everybody was dazed yet relieved. Our neighborhood had not been turned to rubble.

I asked a neighbor what to do, again embarrassed by my lack of preparation for an earthquake in the world's center for such disasters. He told me, "Go home and watch the television."

I headed to meet my wife and friends; we had decided to stick together in case there were further quakes through the night. Walking to the main roads, Tokyo was like I had never seen it. Train stations were empty. We found an open restaurant displaying news.

"You feel different watching news coverage of a disaster if you've been a part of it," my wife said as we walked home a couple of hours later.

Richard Smart
Tokyo

Together

I wasn't there.

I wasn't in the shit. I wasn't grasping my wife's hand in a final expression of love as the Earth violently convulsed. I wasn't watching in horror as the sea reached out, groping, tearing families apart. I wasn't close to the reactors as radiation fears spurred evacuation orders and an exodus of my countrymen from their adopted homeland.

No. I was far away, reading, watching, downloading news of the events 180 miles north. But the quake and all that followed shook me from my expatriate perch. It has cost me nothing more than a single day of work; more a reward than a punishment.

Yet there I was, on the verge of bursting into tears.

Working at a newspaper, seeing the images and reading the accounts of the devastated regions should have been something I was inoculated against. But as the crises deepened, I became increasingly tense. Nuclear plants near the quake's epicenter threatened an uninformed Japanese capital. Aftershocks drove me under tables. I soon couldn't tell if it was me shaking or actual residual tremblors.

As the threat of a nuclear disaster loomed, friends and acquaintances packed up—some leaving Tokyo without an utterance, others professing their guilty consciences to the Internet ether. It was fine. Really, I thought. But the sense of dread it instilled in me was more dangerous to my psyche than any radioactive agent my imagination could conjure up.

Their departures forced me to consider my own. I weighed my options. As a friend said, you'd be a fool not to leave. But I couldn't come up with a solid reason to. I was staying.

Thinking about it now, I can't help but feel guilty. With hundreds of thousands suffering and tens of thousands more dead or missing, what right did I have to feel this way? None, I thought.

But I was wrong. We are all in this together.

Jesse Johnson
Abiko, Chiba Prefecture

Yukiko Kurokawa

Tremors

I left work and got on the train at around 14:40, heading to Shibuya for another train home. Between stations, the train ground to a sudden halt and slammed me into the back of a seat. Initially I thought an accident had occurred, but the driver announced, "Tokyo is experiencing a huge earthquake, please brace yourself." Seconds later, the train shook violently, like a ship on rough seas. It shook from side to side, front to back. Nobody showed signs of panic or distress, except that most people's faces turned very pale.

After this first shock, the train crawled to the next station, Omotesando. I got off, and hesitated as I wondered what I'd find when I got above ground. People seemed calm enough, but many were trying to exit the station since train services had been stopped. When I got up to the street it was swarming with people. A few were crying, but most were waiting in lines to use the public phones, which are free in emergencies. Cell phone coverage had been knocked out.

I realized that I was going to have to walk home, so I headed off in the right direction for the long journey. I had only walked a couple of yards when I heard a group of guys ahead of me shouting, "MOVE! DANGER!!" I looked up and the buildings were moving and swaying. An aftershock hit and I felt the pavement drop and ripple under my feet. People moved quickly to the center of the street. Some people abandoned their cars. The sky turned an ominous black color. I thought this was the "main event."

Luckily, the tremor soon ended and I was able to continue. In Shibuya glass had fallen from high windows on to pedestrians, and there was mass disorder. Two and a half hours later I was home. My house was relatively unscathed, but when I switched on the TV I realized the extent of what had just happened.

Since then, a lot of people have left Tokyo fearing what may come. However, my life is here, and that has almost returned to normal. The situation in Japan is serious, undoubtedly, but people northeast of here have it far worse than I. And I would rather stay and help the people in a country that has embraced of me for a long time.

Iain Hair
Tokyo

Trousers

Three days after the earthquake I found myself accompanying a journalist to the north. After six hours spent locating a can for spare fuel (sold out citywide), and then another couple of hours looking for fuel, we set out on Route 4, destination: Koriyama evacuee center, 70 km south-west of the Fukushima nuclear plant.

As we crawled north on local roads, we saw convoys of Japan Self-Defense Forces vehicles on the motorway beside us. The further north we got, the more quake damage we saw. Houses that had lost their walls. Great fissures across the road. A four-story office block reduced to two.

Arriving at Koriyama we headed to the Radiation Detection Unit, a series of tents set up in a parking lot staffed by men dressed in full-body radiation-proof suits, armed with geiger counters. We had walked onto the set of ET. A father, mother, two children and their dog had just arrived, and one-by-one were checked over. There was a commotion—the father had radioactive trousers. The family rushed back to the car to find a spare pair as he was stripped down and washed. That day, 144 of 4,295 people that had been scanned had tested positive.

We interviewed a few teenagers living with their families in the baseball stadium converted into rescue center there with their families. One said, "I used to hate going to school, but now all I want is to go back, study hard, see my friends. I want my normal life back."

Joseph Tame
Tokyo

Underground

Central Tokyo, Friday, March 11, 2:46 p.m., I was three levels underground waiting for a train and privately hoping for my last business meeting of that day to be short, so I could get home for an early weekend.

It was not to be.

"To all passengers. Please stay calm. The station and platforms have been designed to withstand earthquakes, and you are safe where you are." The stationmaster's panicked voice over the intercom was hardly reassuring. But with the ground under me vehemently trying to sweep me off my legs, it was not as if I had much of a choice anyway. I held on to a signboard and tried to call my wife, waiting for the wave of aftershocks to subdue. When it finally did, I walked the stairs up to the first level. By now, water had started to leak from a crack in the station's ceiling, and suddenly the "You're safe" announcements changed 180 degrees into "Evacuate, now!"

Elevators not working, a mother in front of me was struggling with a baby in a big stroller. I told her to take my bag and hurriedly carried the stroller with its precious content to the daylight.

Outside, the usually quiet park adjacent to our office was literally packed with thousands of people taking refuge, the better-prepared ones wearing hardhats. In the distance the sound of ambulances, and at a particularly large aftershock the sound of breaking glass. Like me, many people were frantically typing on their mobile phones, and I finally managed to get a text message through the overloaded network to my wife, and then to my parents back in Europe.

It was only when, after what seemed the longest of times, I finally received an answer back from my wife, saying she and our children were fine, that I could breathe normally again.

Bigger in Japan
Kamakura

Underneath

Morning, 19 March 2011. Woke up thinking, "Oh my, I slept through a whole night." Then I immediately felt guilty in my bed with enough bedding to keep me warm even without the heat on. Knowing full well this is called survivor's guilt.

What else am I feeling? A constant, nagging dread. Am I afraid? Of course I am. I'm terrified. Am I panicking? Uhh, I don't think so. But compared to my normal state, I suppose I'm rather quietly frantic. I'm a Japanese woman, 45, born in Tokyo. I grew up here and in New York, and eventually went to university in Oxford. In the 1990s I was a reporter for the Asahi Shimbun, a Japanese national daily, and I covered the Hanshin earthquake on the ground in Kobe from day one. Until March 11th, 2011, that had been the most traumatic experience of my life.

On the morning of January 17th 1995, I was about 80 kilometers (50 miles) away from the epicenter of the Hanshin quake. What I felt then was a gigantic bang beneath me, followed by deadly silence. That was the effect of a magnitude 7.3 quake. The data show that the initial tremors lasted for 15 seconds. On the afternoon of March 11th 2011, I was about 350 kilometers (220 miles) from Sendai, the largest city near the epicenter. This time the earth groaned and shrieked, even as far away as that. And it went on and on and on, for what seemed like an eternal five minutes.

I think I thought about death. I don't really remember. That was the force of a magnitude 9.0 quake. I'm not a scientist, but I understand that means that it was 1,000 times more powerful than the Hanshin quake, which killed nearly 6,500 people. I don't ever remember being so constantly afraid. "Then why do Japanese people look so calm?" you may ask. Why so orderly? Why do we insist on queueing? Paying at the cash register? I can't speak for all of us, but those around me, the family, friends, colleagues and university students I know, have all said: "Because that's what we do."

Of course, violent crime and petty theft are commonplace in Japan, as in any other country. I used to cover the police as a reporter, so I know this well. But the majority of us, the people you see going about their daily business despite a sick, sinking feeling in the stomach, don't loot. Neither would you, right?

A few nights ago, I received an SOS e-mail from a high-school friend I hadn't seen in nearly 30 years. She and her husband are doctors in Fukushima. Her husband's family runs a mid-sized hospital and elderly care home outside the evacuation zone. The SOS said the hospital/home was running out of fuel and diapers. I did my best to dig out old government contacts from my days as a reporter, and eventually had someone from the Tokyo government call the besieged hospital to assess their situation.

I understand from my friend that the doctor on call told the government official, "Well, we're all right, I think." My friend was furious and proud at the same time; his answer was so typical of a modest, proud Tohoku man. So to see someone from that region, an elderly gentleman, break down in front of the TV cameras even for a fleeting moment is ...well... I have no words to explain.

The depth of one's emotions is not necessarily proportional to the level of emotion being expressed. I live in Tokyo. As of the morning of March 19th, the incessant aftershocks have abated somewhat, and the fear now is of course the still-burning power plants. In the past week, we have all scrambled to become nuclear radiation experts. Initially after March 11th, I had thought I could more or less project the future chain of events, because we've experienced major quakes and tsunamis before. But I have no clue whatsoever about what may, can or will happen with Fukushima No. 1. I have never felt so helpless about something that might have such a profound effect on the well-being of my family, friends, my compatriots and myself.

Of course I'm terrified.

But we in Tokyo, the people I know, the people I see bustling about in the streets, sitting next to me on the trains, are all going about our lives. Some call us naïve, deluded and foolhardy. Perhaps. But many of us have no other choice. Many people have fled because they could and they wanted to.

For those of us with pets, or with ailing or elderly family members, or with any other circumstance that makes a quick evacuation impossible, the situation would have to become much, much worse before we would make that big push. But that doesn't mean we aren't thinking about it. People here seem to have a constant sick, sinking feeling. I constantly feel dizzy, as if I'm rocking and swaying all the time in a boat on the Cherwell. And this doesn't help at all.

From the outside, we may act calm and cheerful to the point of seeming creepy. But do understand: We are crying inside, we are gritting our teeth, often literally. I seem to have developed a constant crease in my forehead.

I asked a friend the other day, "I wonder if this is a bit like living in a war zone?" She said, "Darling, this IS a war zone. We're just lucky we have no enemy to hate." Right. So I'm now in a war zone. So the streets turn dark at night. Right. We put on extra jumpers and socks to keep ourselves warm. Yes. Well, I can just remember the 1960s, before Japan became a super-rich country. Back then, nights were dark and winters were cold. I feel sorry for the younger people who have only known bright nights, warm winters, and very little material want. They don't know how to react.

But we can teach them, as we wait for the cherry blossoms to come out. And I think I will daydream of the daffodils in Christ Church Meadow. With, of course, a very stiff upper lip.

Yuko Kato
Tokyo

Understanding

My apartment is 5,629 miles from Sendai. At 10:46 PM on Thursday March 10, local time, I was getting ready to go to bed when posts started flooding my Twitter client. My first reply was, "Hey Japan, are you ok? #EarthQuake #GetToHighGround."

I was horrified by the nightmare visions on NHK World's online broadcast: A sea of burning debris pouring across Sendai farmlands, racing up embankments and sweeping houses aside like matchsticks. I started posting to Twitter and Facebook and stayed glued to the live feeds. Days passed.

I can't pretend to have even an ounce of understanding of what the survivors are going through right now, searching debris for missing loved ones, finding parents and children crushed in the rubble of what used to be their homes. Right now there are so many survivors who might die because of inaction. I'm afraid and tired, and I'm worried for my two friends who haven't made contact. But I set aside my own feelings and translate and repost messages by the thousands, hoping that maybe one message will make a difference to one person. Just one.

Useless? Naïve? Stupid? Maybe. But I keep doing it, because the only alternative I have is to stop, and fall apart at the horror of it all.

がんばります (I'll do all I can.)

Mari Kurisato
Denver, Colorado, USA

Values

I've been thinking about lots of things since I married a Sri Lankan. The great earthquake made me realize clearly that in seeking convenience and riches, Japan has been losing sight of the most valuable things. Now is the time to bring back the lost values—bonds, family, love and nature.

Whether Japan can really revive or not depends on that.

Kaoru Raban
Kohoku, Chiba

Vertical

I certainly don't believe any of that "divine retribution" crap, which happens to unify the philosophies of right wing American broadcaster Glenn Beck and right wing Tokyo governor Shintaro Ishihara. But I can appreciate a cosmic joke.

The massive earthquake that hit northeast Japan on March 11th came right in the middle of moving season. The Japanese fiscal year and the school year begins April 1 or thereabouts, and traditionally many people move house during the month of March, because of job transfers, university admission, or because they just like to do what everybody else is doing. Consequently, there were a few trucks outside our 38-story building in the Shitamachi district of Tokyo the weekend after the quake, carrying furniture for folks who were moving in. Fortunately, the freight elevator was operational again by the morning of the 12th, but what did those new arrivals think standing in their new apartment while it swayed back and forth during one of the many aftershocks?

Maybe they had lived in a high-rise before, but in any case the quake helped test a theory, at least partially: Would all these earthquake-proofed structures actually withstand a massive quake? Of course, the epicenter of the one we experienced was a hundred kilometers off the coast of Iwate Prefecture, but according to reports, no buildings collapsed in Sendai, the nearest large city to the quake and one with its own share of skyscrapers. So the technology seems to work, and while it certainly saves lives and property, it doesn't solve a more intractable problem: Once you've been in a large earthquake in a high rise, you don't want to be in another one.

I was writing an email when the quake struck at 2:46. I've lived here on the 24th floor for more than 10 years and been through a good share of quakes. Usually, they start with a disconcerting jolt and then the whole apartment sways gently if sickeningly. From what I understand there are two types of technologies for high rises in Japan. One is designed so that the building is flexible: the entire structure absorbs the energy and disperses it evenly throughout the frame. That means the higher you live, the wider and longer the sway. The other type, which is more expensive, involves spongy shocks in the foundation that absorb much of the energy. We live in the former type. This time, I didn't feel a jolt but rather a

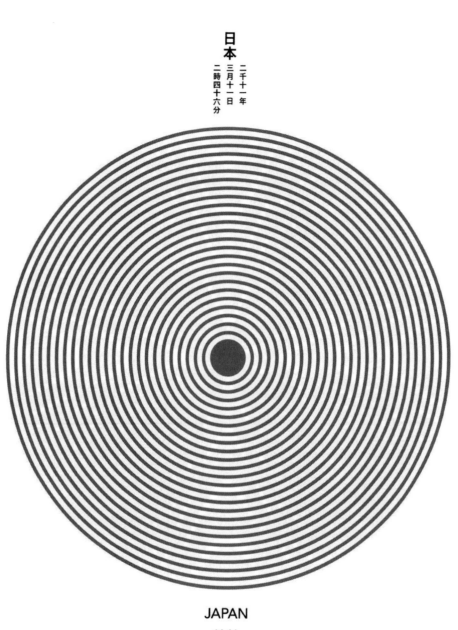

日本
二千十一年
三月十一日
二時四十六分

JAPAN

14.46
11.03
2011

Daniel Freytag

slight rumble from the floor that just kept growing until the walls started rattling violently. Masako knew this was going to be bigger than the usual quake and started sobbing in the next room. We crouched under her desk together as she yelled out for her father (who died when she was 8). The shaking didn't stop. More precisely, it gradually changed to swaying, but the swaying was much broader than in the past. The movement wasn't as terrifying as the noise—a massive creaking sound. And it went on for more than a minute.

A commonly held truism in Japan says that most people who die in an earthquake are crushed by falling furniture. Actually, that's not true: most die from collapsed structures, but the vast majority of these structures are wooden one-family houses. Still, there is something to be said for the falling furniture theory. Because so many Japanese residences have little if any storage space, homes are filled with tall, heavy wardrobes and bookcases, and if they're not fixed to the walls in some way they will fall over. We don't have much in the way of possessions, but the bookcases we bought are the type that attach to the ceiling, so nothing fell over during the quake except a floor mirror in the bedroom, and that didn't break. The TV stand, however, which is on casters, would have moved all the way across the living room if it hadn't been tethered to the antenna outlet.

The only thing damaged in the quake was our peace of mind. Though I now have confidence in the integrity of our building, I don't want to live here any more if it means the possibility of having to go through that again, or worse. Which is a shame, because I like this apartment. It's well laid out, brighter than any place I've ever lived, and the view of Sumida River and the mountains of Nagano and Yamanashi is breathtaking. Of course, an earthquake can be just as scary when you're living on the first floor, but being on the ground is a slightly more reassuring situation, since after it's over you can get out of your building easily. When the shaking stopped, we were basically stuck on the 24th floor. The elevators automatically stop in an earthquake and can't be restarted until a technician arrives to turn them on again, and that could take hours. Having two cats (not allowed, thanks for asking) makes it even more difficult to get out. We have to put them in carriers and then schlep them down 24 floors in a stairwell that may likely be crammed with other people trying to escape. And if we stay, what if the water, gas and electricity are cut off? Or, even worse, a fire breaks out?

These were possibilities we'd considered ever since we moved in here but didn't contemplate seriously until the day after the quake. It may be a safe building, even in a monster quake, but the attendant disadvantages make the prospect of such a quake almost as terrifying as a structural failure.

And one more thing. The so-called building disaster team did nothing after the quake except apologize about the elevator. We live in a UR residence, meaning a semi-public apartment building, which is why the structure was state-of-the-art when it was built. But management is sorely lacking. We have never received literature outlining what we should do in a disaster. Apparently, we are supposed to get that from the public sphere. We're supposed to know that stuff ourselves.

But probably the saddest realization came when Masako went out into the hallway to see if any of our neighbors might need help. Ever since the couple who lived in 2409 moved out a year ago, we don't know anyone else on our floor on anything like a name basis. No matter what you hear about the cohesion of Japanese society, it means less when they reside in a vertical community: they don't even greet one another in the elevator. Even in fear, they keep to themselves.

Philip Brasor
Tokyo

Voices

Growing up with a sibling that was diagnosed with cerebral palsy since childhood is something I can't explain in one word to make you say, "Oh, I totally understand what that's like now." But what I can tell you is the feeling of having my little sister tell me she's jealous of me because I can run in the park, to see her cry in her room, pulling her hair out in frustration with her left hand—the stronger of her two hands. That feeling, that hollowness. Because you are allowed to have, by the powers that be, what someone else (who is no less deserving than you) is denied.

Since March 11th, I've reminded myself that in taking action, it is important to remember that there are many people whose voices in times of emergency are ignored, perhaps more so than they are on a daily basis.

Who will speak for the afflicted elderly, children and disabled, both Japanese and non-Japanese? Where can they go? Who will listen and tell them that their needs are just as important as anyone else's, and begin to address them? Those who have a voice, needing to be expressed—who will make sure that the mouths they come out of are fed, not chapped from cold, not muted by standards of validity or worth?

Jessica Tomoko Perez
The Bronx, New York

Waiting

When my smartphone chimed at 3 a.m. Friday in Ontario, bringing news of a massive earthquake in Japan, I woke Hiromi. Her parents were in Miyagi. She muttered something about calling them in the morning and went back to sleep. We'd spoken to her dad via video Skype only a few hours ago. It could wait.

Morning came, and the TV showed images of cars washing under a bridge like ice floes on a spring river, fishing boats perched atop buildings, entire villages reduced to mud-covered rubble. We called and called to no avail.

We knew Oji-san would have been at home in Wakayanagi, far enough inland to be safe from the deadly waves, but Oba-san was supposed to be in Sendai for a lecture that afternoon.

The barrage of calls from family and friends began almost at once with my parents offering to cut short their southern vacation. "No need," we told them, "there's nothing to be done but wait." I went to work long enough to fill in my boss and was sent home to wait. Hour after hour, we watched the news. We stared at the horror on TV like rabbits on the highway at night, unable to look away from the oncoming headlights. But for us, that doom would never arrive, only constantly approach. All we could do was wait, chained by distance, helpless to act.

Dozens called and emailed to express concern, sympathy, horror and support. Was there anything they could do? Did we need anything? No, there was nothing. Only waiting.

Hours of anxiety stretched into days. The kids were fed at intervals and otherwise left in the care of Nintendo and Walt Disney. I cooked, monitored the news and answered the phone while Hiromi sat glued to NHK's Internet feed and kept up the hourly ritual of dialing through to a recording in Japan telling us our call could not be put through. Appetite and sleep became a distant memory. I'd give in to nervous exhaustion and medicinal vodka and doze fitfully for a few hours, rising to find her maintaining her vigil while the 24-hour cable news drumbeat of despair rolled on.

I stumbled through work, so preoccupied I could barely string a coherent sentence together. Wednesday came and went without contact, the constant worry and not-knowing gnawing at our souls like a trapped rat. We stayed composed, knowing that the least breach of the emotional dam would mean a flood of panic.

Returning from the office early Thursday, I sat down to try to work and saw that my father-in-law's cold, grey Skype icon had turned to bright, friendly green. His computer was back online. They had electricity. I hollered to Hiromi and she dashed to the phone.

We called, and at long last, they answered.

The waiting was over.

Kevin Wood,
Hamilton, Ontario, Canda

Want

I have been around Tokyo for 15 years and I feel I am needed here now more than ever.

The decision whether to stay is the most complex one I have ever had to make in my life. Japan is my adopted home. I would not leave a burning house alone if my family were still inside.

Our house is not as yet on fire but I need to be available in the event it does go up in flames. We as a community don't owe it to Japan. But when I think of the Fukushima 50 risking life and limb, when I think of the children now without parents in the Tohoku region, when I think about the untold damage to the region far beyond the scale of the New Orleans flooding, this is simply where I need to be.

It's where I want to be.

Dan Castellano
Tokyo

Brian Lynn

2011/0

Window

All my Tokyos feel imaginary.

Once, in a cab, whipping along that elevated Tarkovsky expressway, I saw, through an uncurtained window, a man seated naked on the edge of a dark wooden table. Helmut Newton but for real somehow. Of no particular age, with corporate hair. Awaiting something I could not, would never, see, beyond the frame of mullion and concrete. And since then I have tried to fill an infinite depth, of moment, of field, with details I am unwilling to trust. That he was Japanese. Or not. That the table was mahogany, one end of a long dining or perhaps conference table, highly polished. That the room was somehow atemporal, though the décor Occidental (as our grandparents used to say). That he looked at his death, awaiting its approach. Or at some astonishing fulfillment of the heart, unwilling as yet to fully accept its arrival as fact. Or, ditto, some ultimate carnal pleasure. Or, given the night, given this city, the speed of the cab, Japanese cinema and Borges, simultaneously at all three.

"What was the most memorable thing you ever saw in a city?"

"A man, sitting naked on the end of an expensive-looking table. Through a window. In Tokyo. Perhaps the fifth floor. From a cab."

"Where were you going?"

"I have no idea. It was evening, already dark. Near Ark Hills, or just beyond."

"What made it memorable?"

"His stillness." [Becoming evasive] "It's difficult to explain."

The Tokyos I've invented, the fragments of them, and the Tokyos I've seen, the fragments of them. Rattling together now, marbles in a box. Since the earthquake, I have been restless in some very specific way. When I rise from this chair, a part of me wants to go there, to Tokyo. I don't know exactly why. Somehow London and Tokyo are the capitals of my imagination, with Manhattan and Los Angeles like space stations between them. I have lived in none of these places. I doubt I will. Their function is other. Oneiric. Engines of dream.

"'I didn't know whether to scream or shit.'" [Quoting lyrics, the band Television, but this isn't understood, and no doubt makes a strange impression]

William Gibson
Vancouver, BC

Test

The Great Tohoku Earthquake has brought an unprecedented amount of damage in its wake. Something like a magnitude 9.0 earthquake, let alone a large-scale tsunami, was a disaster unimagineable for another 400 years. And then on top of that is the crisis that struck the Fukushima nuclear power plant, leading to radioactive materials being released.

Surely, isn't there something that this latest earthquake disaster, this so-called "triple setback" to our nation, is coercing us to do? For me, I can think of it as nothing less than The Invisible Hand leading us to The Test. Namely, this is The Test of the suffering that compels us to test the strength of our spirits and the limits of our power.

So, what exactly is being tested by this "suffering?" Who exactly? Why exactly?

Along with the victims themselves, countless people are ceaselessly asking, what meaning does this latest, almost unbelievable, suffering carry at its end? Some ask through religion, others through philosophy and still others take it as predetermined fate.

But, for myself, I don't see it as either asking philosophically, or arguing on religious grounds, to say nothing of taking it as mere destiny. The reasoning being that: It Has No Meaning. What is being tested for all of those left is the question: "Can I be a good person or not?" Thusly, what we must think is, what exactly makes a good person?

When they speculated that there might be a shortage, who so shamelessly spent money for unnecessary hoarding?

Who sold currency in the ensuing inflation after the quake?

Did you have fun consciously writing posts fanning the flames of doubt from the comfort of your warm room?

Do you just donate a pittance with a solemn face while leaving the rest for nature to run its course?

Do you only worry about the radiation while putting the land itself at a distance?

Are the victims just others, and not a part of you, too?

In the end, is this all the responsibility of the government?

There are planned blackouts but you're not conserving power, are you?

You complain but you never raise your hand, do you?

You're just waiting until someone decides something, aren't you?

Can you show that type of behavior to children?

"But I'm different!" Are you able to say that?

And if you can say, "I'm different!" just exactly in what way are you different?

Even if it's just a little bit, I think it's fine. Not even completely different is OK, as long as you aren't lying.

For all the forced answers that have been readied, for all the grandiose assertions, all I can hear are mere excuses.

Isn't this test for us to see whether or not we can start to become Good People?

To be a Good Person, it requires neither showy performances, nor great self-assertiveness, nor fancy rhetorical arguments nor any great technique; but instead and rather intangibly, a soft but composed and sincere definition.

One by one, as we stand collectively in this, we can start to define ourselves as Good People.

In our desire to be Good People, a new power and order can take form.

As our unprecedented hardships are ever accelerating, it is a pressing trial on Japan and the Japanese people.

But as we cast each trial off, one by one, who are we to just power down?

As we hold fast to this power and order, can we be made to shift down?

To yourself, myself and all Japanese people, I pray for us all to be Good People.

Yushi Tabe
Tokyo

Andrew Woolner

Acknowledgements

From thinking of the idea on March 18th to finishing the first completed draft on March 25th, took far more effort than I'd imagined. Over 100 people worked on the project, none of whom I had met before. But thanks to Twitter, we were able to form a virtual newsroom that spanned the globe. I would personally like to give my warmest thanks to what quickly developed into the core team of editors—the Colonial Irregulars: Dan Ryan in Brisbane, California, M. Rosewood in New York and Sandra Barron in Los Angeles. This book also owes a massive debt to illustrator and stand-in designer Denver's Mari Kurisato, or Hail Mari as she became known, at least here in the Abiko bunker.

I'd also like to thank Jake Adelstein for staying awake long into the night to complete his article. And where would we be without Yoko Ono's support and William Gibson, who responded with such good humour to my sarcastic tweets cajoling him to join. He even abided by my absurd three-hour deadline. What a pro. What a gent.

But most of all, I want to thank everyone who donated a story or picture. Many didn't make it into this edition, purely from my inability to think and edit fast enough. Without them there could be no book. Finally, may I thank my long-suffering wife who worked tirelessly on this project, gave me love, cups of tea, and a kick when I needed it most.

Our Man in Abiko
25 March 2011

Copy Editors

Lindsey Annison
Sandra Barron
Jesse Johnson
Joanne Greenway
M. Rosewood
Dan Ryan
Owen Schaefer
Jenny Silver
Vania Sofiandi
Aimee Weinstein

Translators

Hiromi Davis
Yoshiko Ikeda
Yuko Kato
Tomomi McElwee
M. Rosewood
Andy Sharp
Yoshie Sherriff
Fernando Ramos
@se7elndn
Shirabe Yamada

Designer

Edward Harrison

Illustrators/Designers/Photographers

James White (Cover design)
Mari Kurisato (Back cover)
Gavin Strange
Linda Yuki Nakanishi
Daniel Freytag
Fernando Ramos
Philipp Christoph Tautz
Brian Lynn
Yukiko Kurokawa
Liza Daly
Samuel Jacoby

Advisors

Kevin Carroll
Roberto De Vido
Jim Bonner
Our Woman in Abiko
Half the blinking planet

Printed in Germany
by Amazon Distribution
GmbH, Leipzig